D1462364

THE MARRIAGE TRACK

Dave & Claudia Arp

A JANET THOMA BOOK

THOMAS NELSON PUBLISHERS
Nashville

OTHER BOOKS BY THE AUTHORS

Almost 13
Beating the Winter Blues
Sanity in the Summertime (co-authored with Linda Dillow)
60 One-Minute Marriage Builders
60 One-Minute Family Builders
60 One-Minute Memory Builders

Published in Nashville, Tennessee, by Thomas Nelson, Inc., and distributed in Canada by Lawson Falle, Ltd., Cambridge, Ontario.

Scripture quotations are from the NEW KING JAMES VERSION of the Bible. Copyright © 1979, 1980, 1982, Thomas Nelson, Inc., Publishers.

Scripture quotations marked NIV are from The Holy Bible: New International Version. Copyright © 1978 by the New York International Bible Society. Used by permission of Zondervan Bible Publishers.

Scripture quotations marked NASB are from The New American Standard Bible. Copyright © 1960, 1962, 1963, 1968, 1971, 1972, 1973, 1975, 1977 by The Lockman Foundation and are used by permission.

ISBN 0-8407-3345-3

Printed in the United States of America

1 2 3 4 5 6 7 — 96 95 94 93 92

To our dear friend and mentor, Vera Mace,
and in memory of her husband, David Mace

CONTENTS

ACKNOWLEDGMENTS

We are grateful to our friends, family members, and participants in our Marriage Alive Workshops whose contributions have helped to make *The Marriage Track* a reality.

Special thanks to our pastor, John Wood, for his biblical input; to Janet Thoma for her encouragement and editorial expertise; to Steve Bjorkman for his creative art that makes *The Marriage Track* fun; and to Susan Salmon and the in-house staff of Thomas Nelson for making the production of *The Marriage Track* fun for us.

PART ONE

GETTING ON THE MARRIAGE TRACK

CHAPTER ONE

Getting Your Marriage on Track

It had been a long, long week. Two Marriage Alive Workshops back to back left us exhausted. It had also been a long, long day. An eight-hour drive was only the beginning. Even more tiring were the hours we had just spent helping parents of four children realize they could survive the adolescent years.

Now, late at night, we drove on this particular narrow, dark, winding Austrian road. All we could think about was getting back to our hotel and hitting the sack, but just at that moment, we hit something else. The sudden jolt and rough ride confirmed our fears—a blowout.

The next morning we were to begin our holidays with a whole week alone in the Austrian Alps. So this was not the ideal time for car problems. It was one of those frigid Austrian nights; our compact rental car was loaded with our luggage and food for our getaway. A flat tire did not fit into our plans, and all that extra baggage didn't help either!

Marriage sometimes reminds us of our Austrian blowout experience. We travel along somewhat overloaded and stressed out. Up the road ahead we keep talking about finding time to regroup and relax, but before we reach that point, we have a blowout. Maybe you haven't experienced a major blowout in your relationship. It's more like a slow, slow leak. You know that if you want to keep tracking together, you need to take some time to work on your relationship, but you just don't know how to get started. We came to that point in our marriage when we made a major move to Europe in 1973. We found ourselves physically together, but emotionally miles apart. Without the ability to speak German, with no close friends and shared activities, and with three small children and no baby-sitters, we found we had lots of time together, but emotionally we felt disconnected. Not that we had a terrible relationship, but over the years the little barnacles on our marriage ship had built up, and we needed to begin cleaning them off. Suddenly we had the time to begin to talk and to face issues that we had been ignoring.

As we stared at each other across the kitchen table, we realized how far apart we had drifted. We didn't even agree about our recent move to Europe. Dave loved the challenge; Claudia missed family and friends. We knew each other so well and at the same time didn't know each other at all. The stress and pressures of moving a family of five (our boys were fifteen months, four and six years old at that time) halfway across the world in six weeks had taken its toll.

The one thing we could agree on was that we needed to get back on track. We loved each other and were committed to our marriage, but the recent move had pushed us apart instead of pulling us together. Have you ever felt that you were just hanging on by one strand? That's how we felt, and it was time to get back to the basics!

A Cord of Three Strands

Fortunately, we agreed that our marriage was a lifelong commitment. We acknowledged that God created and designed marriage. This gave us a strong base upon which to rebuild our relationship. If we were willing to follow His principles, we could get the most out of our marriage—but only if we started with the right premise. We knew that biblical principles for relationships work, and it was time for us to get back to them. Years before we had chosen Ecclesiastes 4:9–12 as our special marriage verses:

> Two are better than one, because they have a good return
>   for their work:
> If one falls down, his friend can help him up,
> But pity the man who falls and has no one to help him
>   up!
> Also, if two lie down together, they will keep warm.
> But how can one keep warm alone?
> Though one may be overpowered, two can defend
>   themselves.
> A cord of three strands is not quickly broken (NIV).

In the past, we had been able to encourage one another—but at this point we were both discouraged. We had always seen the third cord in our marriage as God, and at times like this our faith in God helped us hang in there and get turned around.

That Saturday morning, over two cups of coffee, we began to talk about our relationship and to focus on positive memories. Our conversation drifted back to the time we met. We talked again about what had attracted us to each other—Dave's easygoing personality and listening ear; Claudia's endless ideas and energy. (Somehow after marriage we had redefined this as Dave's being too slow and Claudia's overcommitment and lack of focus.) We talked about our first date and our certainty three weeks later that "this was it!" We found ourselves reliving a long-forgotten part of our lives. And as we focused on the positive memories, we were able to tackle the problems of the present. For the first time we took a good look at our marriage and talked through our relationship—where it appeared to be heading and where we wanted it to go. Then we began to set some bite-sized goals and to work toward each one—step by step. As we reached one, we were encouraged to continue. We hope *The Marriage Track* will help you do the same. We set three basic goals for our marriage and hope that you will consider adopting these goals as well.

Three Marriage Goals

1. Our first goal was to look at and evaluate where our marriage was at the present time. Why not stop right now and look at your marriage? You'll know it's time to regroup and get on track when

> . . . you can't remember the last time you talked for thirty minutes to your mate without phone, Fax, child, door-to-door salesman, or telemarketing interruption.
> . . . your mate calls to say he'll be late for dinner and you have already left a message that dinner is in the oven.
> . . . dating is something you did before you were married.
> . . . the only goals you think about are the ones your child misses on the soccer field.
> . . . your mate spends his free time playing golf and you play tennis (or don't like sports at all).
> . . . your time is filled with overdue projects, car pools, junk mail to sort, bills to pay. Time with your mate? What's that?

Ever Feel Alone?

Think about a couple of times when you felt alone in your marriage. It is possible to be married and still be all alone—to physically close but emotionally miles away—to not be tracking at all. In thinking back over our marriage history, the times we felt most alone and disconnected were the times we were too, too busy! We used to kid about having a front-door relationship. As one of us came in the door, the other left. At that time we had three young children and were both involved in a growing and exciting enterprise. We kept saying that we needed to have more time together and to talk through some issues, but we had difficulty finding that time.

2. Our second goal was to set some long-term marriage goals—to look at where we want our marriage to be in six months, in one year, in five years. As you work your way through *The Marriage Track,* you will have the opportunity to chart your future course and choose your own marriage goals. For now we want you to take a quick glance at the present and the future.

EVALUATING OUR MARRIAGE

Think about how you would want your marriage relationship to grow. Discuss the following topics together.

Three things that are good about our marriage relationship (for example, a great sense of humor, open communication, and common spiritual values):

1. _____

2. _____

3. _____

Two things about our relationship that are good but could be better (like our handling of finances, and sticking to goals that we set):

1. _____

2. _____

One thing I could do to make our marriage relationship better (this is what you can do—not your mate!—like plan weekly one-to-one time or farm out the kids and have a night alone):

1. _____

3. Our third goal was to learn some new skills or learn to use old ones we already knew but didn't use. These skills helped us stay on track and reach our goals. Many times the problem is not knowing what to do, but doing what we know! This process really helped us get turned around. We were able to reaffirm that together we make a great team. We got back on track, but the process took lots of work, and it didn't happen overnight.

Marriage is a journey—not a destination—and today we still work on our marriage. But over the years we discovered principles that helped us build a strong marriage team. As we got our own act together, other couples began to come to us and ask questions. We shared our experiences with them, and before long we were asked to speak to groups about how to build a strong marriage team. After several years, we put together our Marriage Alive Workshop and wrote *Ten Dates for Mates*. For twenty years we have shared these principles and helped thousands of couples build strong, solid marriage partnerships.

We've found that the key to building a successful marriage team is actually taking the time to work on the relationship. Perhaps, like us, you keep waiting to win a two-week cruise for two, for the kids to grow up, or for twenty-four hours of uninterrupted time miraculously to be dropped into your lap complete with coupons for a candlelit dinner for two and a night away at a posh hotel. We would all like gifts like these, but in reality most of us live in a perpetual time crunch. What we need is some way to get our marriage on track and then—though life is hectic—track together. That's why we designed *The Marriage Track* to be simple, practical, and participatory. It's better to discuss together one or two simple concepts than to read passively through a fifty-step discourse on how to have a better marriage. Throughout *The Marriage Track* you will find short, easy exercises. Let us encourage you—do not skip them. Make the time to track together on your marriage.

Whatever your situation—if you're engaged or have been married for many years, if you're a dual-career couple, if you're remarried and have a blended family, if you're parents of little ones or in the empty nest—*The Marriage Track* is relevant to you. Recently we were leading a Marriage Alive Workshop in Budapest, Hungary. At first it seemed awkward to have to communicate through a translator, but once the participants started the exercises and began to talk to their mates and work on their own relationships, we were reminded again that these principles really do work!

What Will It Cost in Time?

Like anything worth doing well, staying on the marriage track requires some time. How to find the time is the question. You can approach this book in any of several ways. One is to set aside time as a couple—like one evening a week or a weekend getaway to build your marriage team. The key to finding the time is to plan and then do!

While *The Marriage Track* is designed to help one couple at a time, it also makes an excellent guide for small groups. If you know yourself and know you need the extra pressure of being committed to others, consider recruiting several other couples and go through *The Marriage Track* together. You might consider getting together once a month as a group to share what you're learning and how your marriage is growing. (A Leader's Guide is available through Marriage Alive International. See Appendix for details.)

Will It Really Make a Difference?

This book will only be helpful if it's used. The difference between reading a book and having your marriage enriched is your involvement! Our goal is to help you enrich and deepen your marital relationship, to get on track with each other and then stay on track!

Research reveals that it takes three weeks to break or start a habit and six weeks to feel good about it. As you work your way through *The Marriage Track,* you will grow in intimacy and actually develop positive patterns of relating to each other.

We're Convinced! How Can We Start?

The first step is to decide together to commit yourselves to creating your own unique marriage track. It really doesn't matter who found the book or whose idea it is. The most important thing is to agree together that you want to enrich your marriage and that you are willing to invest some time to make it happen. A written commitment seems to help us carry through with our good intentions. To help yourself to do just that, fill in the following:

MAKING A COMMITMENT

I agree to invest time in building our marriage and working through *The Marriage Track* with my mate.

Signed: Husband _____

Wife _____

Date _____

The second step is to get out the planning calendar and write in when you are going to do it! We suggest choosing one night a week—for example, every Thursday night at seven. Select a time when you are less likely to have other commitments. One couple we know chose Saturday mornings and went out for an early breakfast. (They were back home before their teenagers ever woke up!)

Our first Tracking Time is _____

We have marked this on our calendar. ___Yes ___No

The third step is to make special arrangements to clear your schedule. If you are a couple without children, this will be easier. If you are parents of young children, you will need to take care of details like arranging for sitters and planning the children's meals ahead. If you both work outside the home this might be a good time for a pizza or Chinese take-out dinner. List the arrangements you need to make in your particular situation.

Special arrangements we need to make (like get a sitter, make reservations, and feed the dog) are:

1. _____

2. _____

3. _____

Let us encourage you to do whatever is needed to make time alone happen. Sometimes you may feel it's just not worth the effort, but—trust us—it is!

What about interruptions, such as sick children or an urgent project at work? We all know that we occasionally have to alter and change our best-laid plans. When this happens, simply reschedule your time together and persevere. Commitment means hanging in there and guarding your time together!

Don't use the excuse, "It's just not possible at this stage of our family life—when our children are older—when this project at work is completed"—add in whatever your "panic situation" is—"we'll have time for each other." Don't kid yourself! It just doesn't work that way. We are now in the "empty nest," and all the time we thought we would have is crowded with "urgent things to do." We have to work just as hard at finding time to concentrate on keeping our marriage tracking as we did at other stages of family life.

Once you've established when your time together will be think of ways to let your mate know you're looking forward to being with him or her. A phone call or note can add to the sense of anticipation.

Now It's Your Turn!

Make a commitment to read the appropriate chapter and think about the exercises you are going to talk about during your time together. Begin positively. It's easy to see a mate's faults before the positive qualities. Remember, this is not a time to air all problems and grievances and dump on each other. If negative areas show their ugly faces, make a note of them and save them for another time. In fact, let us encourage you to stay positive as you work through this book. We challenge you to see problems as obstacles to growth that can be overcome. Be determined to work together as a team.

This is the time to encourage, build up, and appreciate one another—to put some air in your marital tires, to look down the road together with excitement and enthusiasm as you track together. Now, relax and enjoy the opportunity to spend time with your mate—and don't forget to have fun getting your marriage on track!

TRACKING TOGETHER

Getting Your Marriage on Track

Purpose:

To look at our marriage as it is right now

To begin to track together in building our relationship

Preparation:

Review Chapter 1, "Getting Your Marriage on Track"

Fill out exercises and be ready to discuss.

Our Tracking Time is:

Date _____

Place _____

Tracking-together Time:

Together discuss:

1. Evaluating Our Marriage (p. 7)
2. Making a Commitment (p. 11)

CHAPTER TWO

Making Your Marriage a High Priority

What really convinced us to take a couple of days off to attend Dave's twenty-fifth college reunion was a special dinner for all of Dave's fraternity brothers and their spouses. Also, we were going to stay with Eddie, Dave's roommate at Georgia Tech, and Eddie's wife, Janice. We had been in each other's weddings, had lived in the same town, and had kept each other's kids when they were babies. But once both families moved, we lost touch. As we drove to Atlanta, we talked about the great relationship Eddie and Janice used to have and wondered if they had been able to maintain their high-priority marriage.

During the weekend it was easy to pick out those with high-priority marriages, and Eddie and Janice were right at the top—the spark was still there. They had lived in many places—even more than we had—and were then getting ready to move to Minneapolis. Their life was an adventure— they sailed together, loved to travel, and had successfully parented two daughters. Now in the empty nest, they were planning to learn to ski in Utah.

At the fraternity dinner we were amazed at how many of our friends were married—and still to each other. (There were a few young replacements around.) As we renewed old friendships, we observed that some of the couples were obviously still "in love," and committed to their marriage. We wondered about others whose sharp comments to each other and about each other made us rather uncomfortable. Some of the couples whom we remembered being so "in love" in college, seemed not even to like each other now. We wondered—if we could all go back twenty-five years and recapture the romance, would it make a difference in how we related to each other today?

What about you? Maybe the romance has slipped away in your relationship with your mate. We assume at one time it was there! Stop for a moment, and try to remember the time when you couldn't bear to be apart.

A Trip Down Memory Lane

Take a deep breath, forget about the present, and take a trip with us down memory lane.

VISITING MEMORY LANE

Think back into your past. Can you remember the first time you ever saw your mate? (We won't ever forget that day. Claudia was thirteen, and Dave threw her into the swimming pool with her clothes on! But we were first attracted to each other when we met after high school.)

The first time I saw my mate was _____

_____

_____

List three things that attracted you to your mate. (Dave liked Claudia's endless energy and ideas; Claudia loved Dave's easygoing personality and listening ear!)

1. _____

2. _____

3. _____

What do you think attracted your mate to you? (Don't be modest!)

1. _____

2. _____

3. _____

What about your very first date? (We went to the youth group at church where Claudia was speaking and then to a drive-in movie to see *A Summer Place*. No, it isn't what you're thinking. In Ellijay, Georgia—Claudia's hometown—there were no cinemas and we had to drive fifteen miles to Blue Ridge to the drive-in if we wanted to have a movie date!) Now it's your turn.

List things you remember from your first date. (Where did you go? How did you feel? What did you wear?)

Think back to when you first realized that you really cared for each other and that the relationship was going somewhere. How did you feel?

Do you remember the first time you discussed marriage? (The first time we seriously talked about getting married was in the middle of our college years. Our nation was experiencing the Cuban missile crisis. The Russian missiles were headed for Cuba and the U.S. forces had their blockade in position. We were convinced that the world was going to blow up and we might never get to live together as husband and wife! So we just did it! We got married without the benefit of *The Marriage Track* or any of the other great helps available today.)

Put down your memories of the first time you discussed getting married.

Think about the day you got married. (We'll never forget our wedding day. Dave took a nap an hour before the ceremony and would have missed the wedding if his dad hadn't wakened him! Claudia was a different story. She was so nervous that she hardly slept the whole night before!)

How did you feel on your wedding day? _____

_____

_____

_____

_____

What do you remember about your first home? (When we were first married, we lived in a tiny basement apartment. We had to walk up two steps to the bathroom, but the ceiling was the same height as in the rest of the apartment. All the plumbing was under that bathroom floor. We called it our split-level bathroom. It was fortunate that neither of us is tall because our bathroom ceiling was about six feet high. We were both still in college and accepted all hand-me-down furniture. We'll never forget our hand-me-down bed. The slats were too short and our bed kept falling in!)

Describe the first place you called home. _____

_____

_____

_____

Now think about a couple of times you have felt especially close to your mate. It might be the birth of a child, an intimate weekend away, or a walk on the beach. (We still have a little seashell picture we made from shells we picked up during a "special walk.") As you write them down, share what made these times so special with each other.[1]

Name 2 times you especially felt close to your mate.

1. _____

2. _____

Having a High-Priority Marriage

It's fun to think back into our history and remember the excitement of that time when we realized we were "in love." If some of that initial excitement has fizzled, we want to help you rediscover it! We want to help you get your marriage on track! High-priority marriages like Eddie and Janice's don't just happen without work and doing some things right.

In Genesis 2:24 we read, "For this cause a man shall leave his father and his mother, and shall cleave to his wife, and they shall become one flesh" (NASB). In this verse we see three principles basic to a growing, healthy marriage: leaving, cleaving, and becoming one flesh. The importance of these principles is emphasized by the fact that Jesus, though He had very little to say specifically about marriage, directly quoted this Old Testament passage. It appears three times in the New Testament in Matthew 19:5, Mark 10:7–8, and in Ephesians 5:31.

In both Matthew 19:5 and Mark 10:7 Jesus reminds us that the Creator made us male and female and created us in God's image. In this context of being created by God both male and female to complement each other and to mirror His image we are told to leave, cleave and become one flesh. In this chapter we want to consider these three biblical principles for placing a high priority on your marriage. Ignoring any one of them will make it easy to get off track.

1. The Commitment to Leave: "A Man Shall Leave His Father and Mother"

Leaving is a physical act, but it is also an attitude. Many people enter marriage willing to run home to mother at the first crisis; they have difficulty cutting the emotional apron strings. One wife told us: "My husband and I didn't get along well at all in the first months of our marriage. We were living in another town and I remember calling my mother. My husband and I had a ghastly fight and I wanted to go home. My mom refused to let me come (wise mother!). She told me, 'You married him; you've just got to work it out.'"

This wife was in the process of learning to leave. Running home to Mama was not an option—she had to learn alone with her husband how to work things out.

When we were first married, we were still in college. We were both committed to completing our degrees. (This pleased our parents!) They wanted to encourage us but at the same time respected the principle that we needed to be "on our own" with no strings attached. Claudia's parents wisely offered to loan us money for Claudia's tuition. This allowed us to "leave" and separate and start our own team feeling quite independent. Later, after Claudia graduated, they canceled the debt as a graduation present. It was a wonderful gift, but the most valuable gift was that feeling that we had really "left" and were on our own.

Stand beside, but not between. Recently we attended a wedding, and the unique presentation of the couple by both sets of parents impressed us. Because it so aptly pictures the principle of leaving, we asked permission to include that part of their wedding ceremony. It went like this:

> The union of this couple brings together two family traditions, two systems of roots, in the hope that a new family tree may become strong and fruitful. Theirs is a personal choice

and a decision for which they are primarily responsible. Yet their life will be enriched by the support of the families from which each comes.

Celebrant: Will you parents encourage this couple in their marriage?
Parents: We will.
Celebrant: Do you celebrate with them the decision they have made to choose each other?
Parents: We do.
Celebrant: Will you continue to stand beside them, yet not between?
Parents: We will.

This principle of leaving also appears in the traditional wedding choreography when the bride's father "gives her away" and steps back from between them, joining their hands.

Sometimes it's hard for parents to step back and not give advice and interfere. As parents of married children, we realize the role we play in facilitating the "leaving." Fortunately for us, both married sons live at least a day's drive away. The principle of leaving involves refocusing our lives on each other and giving our relationship with our mate a higher priority than other relationships. If you put your career, children, sports, hobbies, or whatever before your mate, nothing you can buy or give your mate will really satisfy.

Do you still need to leave an area in your life, to give it a lower priority than your relationship with your mate? What about your job? Or have you designated a higher priority to your children? What about your hobbies or friends or television? Are you overinvolved in community service activities or even too committed to church activities? We knew one mate who had a different church meeting to attend every night of the week! Unless you are willing to count other relationships and activities less important than your relationship with your mate, you will not experience God's best for your marriage.

But before you feel guilty . . . We all would probably agree that our marriage relationship should be our top priority human relationship, but in days, hours, and minutes sometimes it just doesn't work out that way. We recently talked to a young couple who are parents of three active boys—ages four years and younger. They told us how they "left all the stress" and slipped away to a restaurant but were too exhausted even to talk! Life is a delicate balancing act. Some things we can control; other things we simply must juggle. An excellent book we recommend to help you find balance (without adding more guilt) is *Balancing Life's Demands* by J. Grant Howard (Multnomah).

If we peel off the layers of activities and time commitments, what is underneath? Do you often have wistful thoughts about your mate? Do you use wisely the time you do have? We told our friends with the three small boys that they probably needed to go somewhere and sleep instead of forcing tired conversation over a meal. We suggested that they try to get away for twenty-four hours and even offered to be the milkman for their baby. (The mother is nursing, and we offered to "pick up" her milk and deliver it to her baby son!) We call this "creative leaving."

What about your situation? Stop and apply the principle of leaving to your life. Think back to when you first were married.

THINGS I NEED TO LEAVE

Things I left when I married my mate (like financial security, a more affluent lifestyle, or geographic location):

1. _____
2. _____
3. _____

Things I still need to leave or give a lower priority (like overinvolvement in community volunteer work, job overload, too much time on the golf course or tennis court or in front of the television):

1. _____
2. _____
3. _____

2. The Commitment to Cleave: "And Shall Cleave to His Wife"

What does it mean to cleave to one's mate? Webster's defines *cleave* as "to adhere; to cling; to stick; to be faithful, loyal and unwavering." The principle of cleaving is one of commitment and permanence. Unfortunately, some marriages today model another definition of cleave and that is to "split." We think of a meat cleaver and it's not a pretty picture of marriage! It is the opposite of the meaning of the word *cleave* in Genesis 2:24. In God's blueprint there is no six-months' trial, money-back guarantee on marriage! Unless we are committed to permanence in marriage, it becomes easy to give up when problems come along, and anyone who's been married more than two weeks knows that problems are a given.

The commitment to cleave in our marriage relationship goes beyond a commitment just to stick together. No one wants a mediocre marriage. Cleaving requires acceptance and self-sacrifice. It calls for thinking of the other person and looking for ways to make the marriage team even more united.

Cleaving also means being each other's best friend—being that one person the other can always count on. Stop and think about what you are doing to build your friendship with your mate. Do you share common interests and hobbies? While you benefit from your differences, you also benefit from shared activities. As you go through *The Marriage Track*, you will have opportunities to talk about things you would like to do together. In a growing, healthy marriage, partners are friends and continually look for ways to cleave to one another.

Our marriages are never static; they are always changing—either growing or withering. When we ignore the cleave principle and forget to concentrate on building our marriage team, it's easy to get bored. We cover up by becoming overinvolved in work, and that leaves less time to work on our marriage relationship. Researchers tell us that the number one cause of divorces today is failure to work on the marriage.

Our own informal research shows that the number one reason couples don't work on their marriages is lack of time! A close second reason is that couples are bored with their marriages and fill up their time with other activities or their work—which comes full circle to keep them from investing time in their marriages. The time you invest right now in *The Marriage Track* will help you overcome boredom and build an enriched and fulfilled marriage relationship.

We all have daily opportunities to apply the cleave principle to our marriage relationships. The daily pressures of life, the hard times as well as the good times, can help to glue us together. The key is to pull together instead of pushing apart. Are you loyal and committed to your mate? Do you support your marriage team?

PULLING TOGETHER OR PUSHING APART?

Let's get specific. What types of things tend to pull you together? List them. (For us, our work in marriage and family enrichment pulls us together as well as our common faith in God.)

1. _____

2. _____

3. _____

These are the things you want to do together as much as possible.

What things tend to push you apart? List these as well—like finances, time pressure, discussing inlaws, disagreeing about the children. (For us yard work is not a good subject!)

1. _____

2. _____

3. _____

These are negative situations. Avoid them as much as possible.

When you have a choice to make, ask yourself, "Will this action or attitude bring us closer together, or will it put distance in our relationship?" When we have left our child-hood homes and are cleaving to our mate, we have the won-derful opportunity to truly become one.

3. The Commitment to Becoming One Flesh: "And They Shall Become One Flesh"

Not only are we to be friends, but just as importantly, we are to be lovers. Along with leaving and cleaving, we are to become one flesh. God designed the sexual union in mar-riage to be a fulfilling, enjoyable expression of love between husband and wife. He created us male and female, and aren't we glad? Again we see the wisdom of His plan in mak-ing us male and female—He created us different from each other. He designed us to complement each other and to expe-rience unique oneness with each other through the sexual union within the bonds of marriage. In Chapter 7 we will look more closely at how we can be creative lovers and be-come one flesh.

Oneness in marriage also gives the picture of two per-sons joining their lives to form a marriage team—growing in intimacy in all areas, enjoying one another completely. Any help we offer our mate helps our team. Any pain, hurt, in-sult, any lack of support or faithfulness, any failure to help our mate will reflect back on our team. We can be the most positive reinforcing human agent in our mate's life and our mate in ours if we are willing to follow these three principles of leaving, cleaving, and becoming one.

Marriage Is a Partnership

When our goal in marriage is to be a team, both part-ners must be willing to share the load, to build a partner-ship. It doesn't happen automatically. Marriage is a process. Like a soccer game, there are no time-outs. A priority mar-riage is not a one-time decision, but a daily choice. We daily choose to leave, cleave, and be one. We still are complete individuals; we still care about others, our careers, our family and friends; but daily we choose to make our marriage the key relationship in our lives. We need to remember these three principles for our marriage and continue to practice them when our children grow up and get married.

The Birthday Setup

We were reminded of this on Jonathan's first birthday away from home. He was a freshman in college and his brother, Joel, and sister-in-law, Jeanne, lived in the same Midwestern town. The week before, we called Joel and Jeanne and suggested they get together with Jonathan on his birthday. At the time, we didn't realize we offended them. They saw us as the hovering parents, making sure they would not overlook Jonathan's birthday. (History says this was a realistic possibility.) We talked to Jonathan on his birthday and were pleased to hear that he had been invited to eat dinner with Joel and Jeanne.

The plot thickens. Our kids talked during the birthday dinner about their irritation with us for checking on them, and they decided to set us up. When we called Jonathan the next day, he said they stood him up—no one was there when he went for his birthday dinner. It was a very sad story.

A couple of days later, we could resist no more and called Joel and Jeanne, only to find out they had actually had the dinner with Jonathan. We didn't appreciate the setup—*irked* might describe our reaction a little more accurately. Claudia, in our defense, told Joel, "We asked because we cared."

He replied, "Mom, it's okay to care, but we're adults, and your 'caretaking' days with us should be over." It hurt to be set up by our own kids, but we realized that our married kids need space to "leave, cleave, and be one together." It was a reminder to us that though we love our family, our marriage team is just the two of us and the Lord. To be strong, our cord must have only three strands.

Where are you in the process of leaving, cleaving, and being a strong marriage team? Are you the young married couple who are striving to remember birthdays on your own? Are you the partners who are sandwiched between married children and aging parents? Are you in the energy crunch of the toddler years or parenting adolescent years? Wherever you are, we encourage you to stop and determine to make your marriage a high priority. Now is the time to leave, cleave, and become one flesh. Now is the time to grow together in intimacy! Now is the time to make your marriage a high priority.

TRACKING TOGETHER

Making Your Marriage a High Priority

Purpose:

    To reaffirm our commitment to our marriage

    To understand three basic principles of a growing
        marriage:

        Leaving (breaking away)

        Cleaving (becoming best friends)

        Becoming one flesh (becoming lovers)

Preparation:

    Review Chapter 2, "Making Your Marriage a High
        Priority"

    Fill out exercises and be ready to discuss

Our Tracking Time is:

    Date and Time _____

    Location _____

What needs to be done to make it happen:

    1. _____

    2. _____

    3. _____

Tracking-together Time:

    Together discuss the following exercises:

    1. Visiting Memory Lane (p. 16)

    2. Things I Need to Leave (p. 23)

    3. Pulling Together or Pushing Apart? (p. 26)

CHAPTER THREE

Finding Unity in Diversity

It is amazing how two people can live together for many years and yet look at life from such different perspectives. Consider our friends who wrote us about their trip to Europe:

> In thinking of writing about our trip, I read over Ed's notes and thought we would combine our diaries, but now I wonder if we made the *same* trip. He remembers how far it is from Stockholm to wherever, what the money exchange was, what we had for breakfasts, how many meals were on our own, and the address of every airline office in the four countries. It is really a truism that opposites attract and that God puts different people together in order to bring out the best—worst—in them. So if you want to know how far north or south we went, ask him. I have no idea! The nearest we ever came to divorce was once when we were going to New York by car— he was driving and I was the copilot (the only time!). I had the map upside down and we were going merrily south when he wanted to go north!

Do you ever wonder if you're on the same trip as your mate? We agree with our friend who confirmed in her travel experience that "opposites attract." However, the very characteristics that attracted you to your mate—his or her easygoing nature, never in a hurry, always has time for people—may later be an irritation.

Discovering Our Team

We are very different from each other, and sometimes the differences not only attract us to one another but also create tension in our relationship. For the first eight years of our marriage we tried changing the other, and it just didn't work. Dave didn't understand why Claudia couldn't just "laugh things off" and not take life so seriously. Claudia wanted Dave to be more introspective and analytical.

And then we made a job change that required us to take a battery of psychological tests. We still remember the day we filled out those tests. Dave nonchalantly checked off his answers while watching a football game on television. Claudia was intense, cross-checking her answers for "consistency."

The next week we were interviewed by Dr. Blaudau, a psychologist. He sat at his desk, looking at our test results. "Dave, here are your strong points." As he listed them, Dave began to feel better and better. He went on, "Now here are the areas in which you are weak." That wasn't nearly as enjoyable for Dave to hear, but the psychologist was right on target!

Then he went through the same procedure with Claudia, listing her strengths and weaknesses. Looking at both of us he said, "Dave and Claudia, here are the areas you agree on, and here are the areas in which you tend to have problems." He could have been a fly on our walls the past year—he didn't miss anything. Our respect for those psychological tests went up about 300 percent. Then he gave us one of the most beneficial challenges of our lives: "You probably noticed, Dave, that your weak areas are Claudia's strengths, and, Claudia, your weak areas are Dave's strengths. If you will allow each other to operate in your areas of strengths and not be threatened by the other, you have the potential for being a terrific team."

We would like to say that we went right out and applied his advice instantly—but it didn't happen quite like that. It's hard to admit openly that your weakness is your mate's strength and vice versa. It took time and practice, and at times it seemed really awkward, but we took Dr. Blaudau's challenge seriously. We knew if we could follow his advice we would be a stronger team.

The Newsletter Dilemma

One of the first attempts to apply this principle was in writing our newsletters. For years we have sent out a newsletter several times a year to those interested in our work. Getting the newsletter written and out had become a real source of frustration and conflict. Writing newsletters was not one of Dave's favorite activities, and for some reason (still unknown to us) Dave was chosen for that task. Claudia's gentle and not-so-gentle prodding did not help motivate Dave to write it. Once he finally sat down to write the newsletter, he went on and on, ending up with a newsletter crowded with too many details and pages too long.

When the letter was finally finished, Dave, having a real sense of accomplishment, showed it to Claudia. She gave her opinion freely: "It's much too long. Why did you include this part? Delete this. Here, I'll help you." At that point, the only help Dave wanted was to be left alone. He knew Claudia was gifted in writing, but he wasn't benefiting from her strength. After our interview with the psychologist, when time to write a newsletter came around again, we reevaluated our strategy. If writing was one of Claudia's strengths, why not switch and let Claudia do the basic writing? Together we discussed the main content we wanted to include in the letter. Then it was Claudia's turn. Amazingly, she actually enjoyed getting it down on paper. Dave was much more the detail person, so he took over getting it printed, envelope stuffing, stamping and mailing. Personally, he had been frustrated in the past when Claudia bought plain stamps. To her a stamp is a stamp is a stamp. But to Dave, the detail guy, the most appropriate stamp was best. (In February, the stamp would say "love" or at least have a heart on it. Other times our stamps are color coordinated to go with our stationery.)

The result of our initial experiment to concentrate on each other's strengths? First, our newsletters improved. Secondly, our relationship improved. As we both used our strengths, we learned from each other. Over the years, Dave has learned to put his thoughts down on paper better, and now we write books together. Claudia has learned to handle details a little better, and if she's buying the stamps, she even looks at the various designs.

Balancing Our Finances

We have also really worked on our finances. We had already been through "Dave does it all" and "Claudia does it all"—the latter being a real disaster! We didn't always agree on just how our finances should be handled and once again experienced tension and frustration in our relationship. Could we benefit from trying to balance our strengths and weaknesses? First, we evaluated our strengths and gifts in financial management. Dave comes from an engineering background; he could put all those math courses to work—so he started doing the basic accounting. Being a detail person, balancing the checkbooks, paying bills, and figuring our income tax returns became his domain. This didn't mean Claudia had nothing to say about our finances or that she didn't keep an accurate record of checks she had written (at least most of the time!).

Claudia does participate in the family finances by helping to create a workable, practical budget. Also she knows better than to send Dave to the grocery store. The last time he went on his own, he came home with fifteen cans of soup and all his favorite munchable snacks and without the milk and bread. Over the years Claudia has learned to stretch our clothing and household dollars and somehow or another find fantastic sales and deals.

Do we always agree about our finances? Of course not—if we agreed on everything, one of us would be unnecessary—but we have learned to communicate, compromise, and work out an agreeable game plan for how we earn, save, give, and spend our money. It has definitely been a plus for us to work together as a team, especially in our finances.

Pick Your Strengths

Let us encourage you to assess your strengths and weaknesses, and encourage each other to operate in areas of strength as much as possible. Batteries of psychological tests are not required to determine your basic strengths and weaknesses. However, if you have the opportunity to take them, we would encourage you to do so. We can recommend several:

The Myers-Briggs Type Indicator
The DiSC Test
The Couple's Brain Map
The book, *Please Understand Me*
Taylor-Johnson Temperament Analysis
Marital Evaluation Checklist™ [1]

We want to help you begin to identify the strengths of your marriage team. Different strengths can give balance to your team if you can appreciate those differences and not feel threatened by them. It is natural to feel threatened by the unknown. In areas where you are alike, you may have to look for ways to achieve balance.

WAYS WE ARE DIFFERENT AND ALIKE

Stop right now and think about ways you are different from each other. (For instance, as you have probably surmised, we are very different from each other. Dave is laid back and easygoing; he loves nighttime. Claudia is more activity and time oriented and thinks the day is half over at nine in the morning.)

List ways you are different.

1. _____
2. _____
3. _____
4. _____

Now list ways you feel you are alike. (For example, we have similar values and a common faith in God. We're adventuresome and spontaneous and like to pioneer new things.)

1. _____

2. _____

3. _____

4. _____

Do you already see some areas where your differences give balance to your marriage team? Is there an area where you are so similar that it might be a liability? (For instance, if neither of you is time oriented, you may have to work hard to be punctual.)

Discovering Your Team

Our goal is to build a strong marriage team—to benefit from each other's strengths and appreciate each other's differences. To help us do this, let's look at several continuums that diagram a few of the many human polarities.

But first, a word of caution: Listen to what we don't mean. First, we are not saying that one side of the continuums is better than the other side. Both perspectives on any of the continuums have strengths and weaknesses, advantages and disadvantages. Which side you or your mate tends to be on is less important than understanding that people are different. Determine where you are as a couple, and then as a team take advantage of several ways to balance each other.

Second, we are not saying that men are on one side and women are on the other. While there may be some tendencies, depending on the culture, people are just too complicated to be pigeonholed.

Third, we are not saying that you stay at one place on these continuums and never vary or change. In some groups, for example, a person may be very extroverted and at other times quiet and introverted!

BALANCING OUR SEESAWS

While we realize that human personality and relationships are incredibly complex, the following exercises can enhance your understanding of yourself, your mate, and your relationship. Place yourself and then your mate on each continuum. Think of the continuum as a seesaw, and consider how you might balance each other. The first continuum we will look at is Feelings-Facts.

Feelings Oriented/Facts Oriented

Feelings-Oriented Person: The feelings-oriented person tends to express feelings and emotions. He or she likes an open atmosphere, and if tension enters the relationship, the feelings-oriented person strives to clear the air. There is a desire to work through conflict and "not let the sun go down on" anger. This person needs feedback from the other. The feelings-oriented person is more relationship oriented than facts oriented.

Check yourself. Initial what describes you. Now initial what describes your mate.

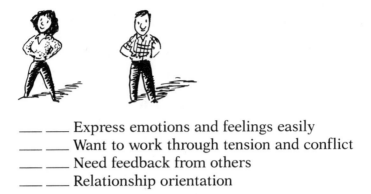

___ ___ Express emotions and feelings easily
___ ___ Want to work through tension and conflict
___ ___ Need feedback from others
___ ___ Relationship orientation

Facts-Oriented Person: The facts-oriented person approaches life from a more cognitive perspective. This person speaks to express ideas and to communicate information more than to express feelings. He or she would rather not face unpleasant feelings and even becomes uncomfortable when emotional subjects arise, preferring peaceful coexistence to being confronted with emotions. This person is more goal oriented than people oriented. Our friend Ed tends to be facts oriented. He recalls the events of the trip. His feelings-oriented wife is amazed at the facts he remembers.

Again, check yourself. Then check your mate.

___ ___ Like to deal with facts and structures
___ ___ Uncomfortable dealing with emotions and feel-
ings

_____ _____ Like to avoid conflict
_____ _____ Cognitive and logical

How This Can Help

Suppose you are trying to reach a solution in a certain situation. One of you is more facts oriented and the other is more feelings oriented. Rather than creating a problem, your different perspectives can be beneficial. If a decision is made purely on feelings, you may be in for trouble. On the other hand, if the decision is based entirely on cognitive information, you may be ignoring important input. What can help you achieve a balanced solution is to identify where you are both coming from. Stop right now and place yourself on this continuum:

FEELINGS-ORIENTED   FACTS-ORIENTED

Now place your mate. Do you balance each other on this "seesaw"? For example, Dave is actually a little more feelings oriented than Claudia, who lives more on the fact-orientation side. In relating to others, Dave is sensitive to what's going on emotionally. It was much easier for Dave to identify with our children—especially during their teens—while Claudia, with her cognitive approach, kept our ship moving forward. As parents and partners, we discovered we make our best decisions together. Both perspectives are important! If you are both feelings oriented or facts oriented, how can you compensate for that? (For example, if you are both feelings oriented, it's easy to get caught up in the excitement of the moment and overlook facts, like the couple who were shopping for a new car. They both got "carried away" and committed themselves to buying a new car on a used-car budget. They both ignored their financial reality and ended up with large car payments that drained their limited budget. They have already decided that the next time they shop for a car, they will compensate for their weakness by doing their financial homework and deciding just how much they can spend *before* they hit the car lots.)

Now note how you compensate if you are alike.

_____

_____

_____

If you are opposites, how can you balance each other?

_____

_____

_____

Private/Public

Another continuum to consider is the private-public continuum. The private mate likes to be alone and to have time alone as a couple. Privates shy away from "groupie" types of things. A young couple who recently attended a Marriage Alive Workshop, Jay and Laura, are both "privates." They would love to live on a desert island and have little interest in others. Jay and Laura naturally protect their private time together, but to achieve balance on this continuum, they needed to be encouraged to get involved with others. They might take the initiative in joining a couple's group or a bowling league, or they could make a list of people they would like to get to know better and occasionally invite a couple over for dinner or dessert. Check yourself by initialing what describes you. Then initial what describes your mate.

___ ___ Like to have time alone
___ ___ Seldom participate in group activities
___ ___ Seldom have others in our home
___ ___ Get tired of being around other people

Kelly and Mike, another couple at the same workshop, were just the opposite. Both are "publics." For them, the more people the better. What's a vacation without friends along? They are both energized by others, care deeply for others, and are involved in other people's lives. To achieve balance on this continuum, Kelly and Mike need to plan time alone. Relationships are built in twos, and they need to be sure to plan enough "two" time to keep their relationship healthy and growing. Again, check yourself. Then check your mate.

___ ___ Like to be around people
___ ___ Prefer group activities to being alone

___ ___ Often have people in our home
___ ___ Seldom have "just two" time

Carl and Sandy are at opposite ends of the continuum. Carl loves people and is continually inviting others to be a part of meals, vacations, trips—you name it. Carl likes to have people around! Sandy's private and just wants to be with Carl. One of her favorite tricks is to "kidnap" Carl for an overnight getaway. Carl and Sandy have to work to find a good balance without one person's orientation overpowering the other. They need to compromise. If they do, they will find balance between being too involved with others and no involvement at all!

Now it's your turn. Place yourself on the continuum. Then place your mate.

If you are both privates or both publics, how can you compensate? (For instance we, at times, get overinvolved with others and have to plan in "just two" times. Sometimes we review the previous month's calendar to check and see how we're doing. Then we use this data as a guide for planning the coming months.)

_____

_____

If you are opposites, how can you balance each other? (For instance, each plan one activity for the next few weeks. One might choose having friends over for dinner one evening and the other plan a date just for two to go hiking on a lonely path.)

_____

_____

Spontaneous/Planner

The Arps are both the spontaneous type. Planning isn't as exciting! Our Marriage Alive board of directors are repeatedly helping us to focus. If left to our own devices, we like to do things spur of the moment. We have to force ourselves to set objectives and do detailed planning.

What about you? Where are you on this continuum?

SPONTANEOUS   PLANNER

If you are both spontaneous or both planners, how can you compensate? (For instance, if you're both spontaneous, you could agree to check with each other before committing yourself and/or your mate to anything else, or if you're planners, you could try to surprise your mate with a surprise activity. One of you will plan it, but it will be spontaneous for the other!)

_____

_____

If you're opposites, how can you balance each other? (For instance, the planner can defer to the spontaneous one, who says, "Why cook dinner tonight? Let's go out to eat." On the other hand, the spontaneous mate can agree to sit down and write out plans for the next week—"Next Friday we'll grill fish.")

_____

_____

Active and Fast/Methodical and Calm

Claudia is the activist. Her definition of "boring" is nothing to do. She doesn't like to take naps during the day—she might miss something. Dave would much rather "let life happen." He marches to a slower (but consistent) drummer. He is methodical and persistent and likes to cross all the _t_'s and dot all the _i_'s. On this continuum we really benefit from each other's perspective and reach a reasonably good balance—most of the time.

To see what your tendencies are, check the following statements that describe you. Then check the ones that describe your mate.

___ ___ Life is action! I don't like sitting still.
___ ___ A nap is one of the spices of life.
___ ___ I like the broad stroke. Details will take care of themselves.
___ ___ Crossing the _t_'s and dotting the _i_'s makes life run smoothly.

Now place yourself and your mate on the continuum:

ACTIVE
AND FAST

METHODICAL
AND CALM

If you are both active or both methodical, how can you compensate for that? (For instance, do you need to slow down or accelerate? Do you need to cut your eighteen hour day or speed up a little bit?)

_____

_____

If you are opposites, how can you balance each other? (For instance, one way we balance each other is Dave sees we keep up with the details like getting the bills paid while Claudia keeps us moving toward the big picture and might say, "Let's look more closely at our fall schedule.")

_____

_____

Night Owl/Day Lark

Why do night people tend to marry day people? It does help you survive the baby and teenage years. The night owl gets the night duty. We have struggled in this area and have been through the "let's change the other syndrome" with no effect at all. Psychologists tell us we are born with an innate time orientation.

What is your orientation? Ask yourself this question: When is your most productive time of the day?

____ ____ Morning
____ ____ Afternoon
____ ____ Evening

This continuum is probably the easiest to identify but the hardest to balance. Over the years we continue to work on harmonizing our "clocks." Claudia's eyes automatically close about the time Dave's pop open. His creative time is between 11:00 P.M. and 2:00 A.M. while Claudia's best time is early in the morning when Dave says, "No one in their right mind should ever get up that early!"

One benefit we have found to being opposites in this area is that it automatically provides a little space in our relationship. We work closely together for long hours. Sometimes it's actually fun for Claudia to slip off to bed early and for Dave to delve into one of his midnight projects. What about your team? Where do you fall on this continuum?

NIGHT OWL   DAY LARK

If you are both night owls or both day larks, how can you compensate? (Many times your job or circumstance will do this for you. One of our night-owl friends is also a surgeon who must arise early for surgery or to make hospital calls. His wife, also a night owl, tries to adjust her schedule. On vacations and off-the-job-times they can stay up all night and sleep all day!)

_____

_____

If you are opposites, how can you balance each other? (For instance, it worked great for us, especially when we had teenagers. It was easy for Dave, the night owl, to stay up until they arrived home. Claudia was bright and cheery whenever one of our boys had to get off on an early school or sports trip. It also helped us to realize that we were different and that we weren't going to change the other—no matter how hard we tried!)

_____

_____

Time Oriented/Not Time Oriented

Here is another continuum where the Arps are different. While we have found some benefits, we've also had to manage lots of irritations. Now if we could just be like our son, Jonathan . . . He went all the way through high school without a watch—yet he was always on time for work, school, whatever! We still haven't figured him out!

Claudia lives by the clock. Once her watch stopped about ten minutes before she was to leave for an appointment. She kept checking her watch and was so tied into her timepiece that she didn't realize for at least half an hour that it wasn't working.

Dave is the classic "nontimed" person. Like the popular author, Garrison Keillor, he's just "happy to be here."

Time—what's that? Time used to place stress on our marriage until Claudia hit upon the ideal solution. She gave Dave a watch with three alarms, and at times he used all three!

We do learn from each other. Claudia has relaxed and sometimes is even ten minutes late instead of ten minutes early. We both make it to weddings on time, and Dave has graduated to a watch with one alarm! There is hope! Where are you on this continuum?

TIME ORIENTED   NOT TIME ORIENTED

If you are both time oriented or both not time oriented, how can you compensate for that? (For instance, if you are not time oriented, alarm clocks, alarm watches, notes to yourself, and—if you're fortunate—an efficient secretary, may help.)

_____

_____

If you are opposites, how can you balance each other? (For instance, we talked through different kinds of situations, and for those most important—like getting to weddings on time—Dave agreed to try hard to be punctual. For others not so important, Claudia tried not to be such a clock watcher.)

_____

_____

_____

Our goal in marriage is not to be the same; we were created with differences. But our goal is to accept each other and benefit from differing strengths. If you find that one of you dominates on most of the continuums, it's time to re-evaluate. Balance is a wonderful concept—especially in a marriage team. It takes work and a lot of patience, but it is worth the effort to find unity in diversity!

Log Removal

What often happens when we see differences in our mate is that we react negatively. This is the natural way, but God has a better way. Matthew 7:3–5 says: "And why do you look at the speck in your mate's eye, but do not notice the log that is in your own eye? Or how can you say to your mate, 'Let me take the speck out of your eye,' and behold, the log is in your own eye? You hypocrite, first take the log out of your own eye, and then you will see clearly enough to take the speck out of your mate's eye" (Arps' paraphrase).

Often we are so concerned with our mate's different perspective that we cannot see our own inappropriate reaction! We suggest the following exercise:[2]

LOG REMOVAL

Step One: List your mate's differences from you that trigger an inappropriate response in you. Make two columns on a sheet of paper. In the left column, list all of your mate's differences that trigger a reaction in you. In the right column, list your inappropriate responses to those differences. Perhaps your mate is not time oriented and tends to be late. Do you assume automatically that your mate just doesn't care or is trying to annoy you by not being punctual? What is your response? Do you lecture, sigh, or start the silent treatment?

As you do this exercise, you may find that your responses are worse than your mate's differences. After you have finished, admit your negative attitude to God and burn or tear up the paper. Do not show it to your spouse; this exercise is for your benefit to help you get the log out of your own eye! The following example may help.

Differences in my mate that trigger my reaction	*My Inappropriate Responses*
1. Not time oriented so he's often late	1. Belittle
	2. Sigh or moan
	3. Nag
	4. Compare with others
	5. Criticize
	6. Neglect
	7. Reject as a person
	8. Be cool sexually
	9. Get angry
	10. Tear down
	11. Be bitter
	12. The silent treatment

Step Two: Admit to God your inappropriate responses and attitudes. In 1 John 1:9 we read, "If we confess our sins, He is faithful and just to forgive us our sins and to cleanse us from all unrighteousness." Remember, the emphasis here is on our inappropriate responses and attitudes, not on our mate's differences.

Step Three: Accept your mate with his or her strengths and weaknesses. Have you ever thanked God for your mate's strengths and weaknesses? If not, do it now. Remember, your mate's temperament can complement your own. It is impossible to change another person; only we can change ourselves. And when we concentrate on correcting our outdated and/or inappropriate responses and attitudes, wonderful things often happen. Others tend to change in response to us! So don't try to change your mate. Concentrate on being the person your mate needs to make your marriage team strong. It is your job to help your mate be happy; trust God to make him or her holy.

Step Four: Ask your mate's forgiveness for your past inappropriate responses. No relationship can thrive without forgiveness. No marriage is perfect; we all blow it from time to time. Relationships are like potted plants: The pot can be broken, but if the plant is repotted and the roots are not left exposed, if it is watered and given tender loving care, it will continue to grow and thrive. Forgiveness is a vital part of marriage. Without it, relationships die—like the potted plant left with its roots exposed. If your mate asks you for forgiveness, give it! The director of a mental hospital said that half of his patients would be able to go home if they were forgiven and knew they were forgiven.

How to Say You're Sorry

If you need to ask for forgiveness for your inappropriate responses and attitudes, do it in the right way. Deal only with what you have done wrong, not with your mate's differences. For example: "Honey, I was wrong to nag you and to pout about being late to church. Will you forgive me?" *Not:* "I'm sorry that I nagged you about being late to church, but you know you're wrong to always make us late!" Remember, you are pointing the finger at your inappropriate response. Don't use this moment as an opportunity to attack your mate. If you attack your mate, you're attacking your own marriage team! (In the next chapter we will be looking at how to communicate effectively without attacking each other.)

A word of caution: If you find you need to go through the process of log removal, do not share your list with your mate. This exercise is a private one, just for you, to get the log out of your own eye!

Get on Your Mate's Team

After you have gone through the steps of log removal (if needed), it's time to get on your mate's team. You are the one who needs to build up the other. You can be the most positive reinforcing agent in your mate's life! After you clear the air, it will be fun to be a team together. Have you discovered areas in which you are too much alike? Are you too opposite in some areas? (For instance, are you all action oriented while your mate is methodical and calm?) On our team Claudia's creativity is balanced by Dave's practicality. Dave's persistence gives continuity when Claudia's burst of enthusiasm and energy runs out! His calmness and fun side add balance to our team. Amazingly, we discovered our greatest assets are our differences! What about you?

After completing this exercise in our Marriage Alive Workshop, one couple told us, "In our twenty-eight years of marriage we have never heard about being a team. This is revolutionary! We have become so bogged down in our individual roles—you know, husbands do this and wives do this—that we've missed benefiting from the strengths of our team. You've also challenged us to concentrate on the positive and see our differences as assets. We've got lots of work ahead, but thanks to this workshop, we're on the right track!"

Another workshop participant questioned us: "We've spent all this time looking at our strengths. . . . When do we get to talk about the weaknesses of our mates?" We used to do both, we explained, but one workshop experience made us reevaluate the benefits and liabilities of listing the weaknesses of the other. We'll never forget the time one husband approached us and said, "We've got a real problem in our marriage—I have all the strengths and my wife has no strengths, only weaknesses! Does this mean I'm supposed to do everything?"

Try as hard as we could, we were unsuccessful in helping this husband appreciate his wife's differences. He was on a negative track and refused to get off. Over the years, his wife had been beaten down, and her sense of self-worth was below zero. His negativeness had helped to derail their marriage, and a weekend workshop was inadequate to put it back on track.

Concentrating on our weaknesses is like poking an open sore. It doesn't bring healing. Over the last twenty years of our marriage enrichment seminars, we have observed that we help much more by concentrating on couples' strengths and helping them see the combined assets of their teams. When we do this, an amazing thing happens. We learn from each other.

Psychologist Revisited

We began this chapter by telling you about our experience with the psychologist and those batteries of psychological tests. Years later, we had the opportunity to retake them and to sit down again with the same psychologist. We were surprised and pleased to learn that we actually had learned from each other. Our weak areas were not as weak. We were a stronger team. We had proven it works! We challenge you to prove it for yourself. Work for unity in your diversity, and you too can be a strong marriage team.

TRACKING TOGETHER

Finding Unity in Diversity

Purpose:
> To understand the basic differences in people
> To understand our strengths and how we fit together
> as a team
> To deal with my past inappropriate responses toward
> my mate

Preparation:
> Review Chapter 3, "Finding Unity in Diversity"
> Fill out exercises and be ready to discuss

Our Tracking Time is:
> Date and Time _____
>
> Location _____

What needs to be done to make it happen:
> 1. _____
> 2. _____
> 3. _____

Tracking-together Time:
> Together discuss the following exercises:
> 1. Ways We Are Different and Alike (p. 36)
> 2. Balancing Our Seesaws (p. 38)
> 3. Log Removal (p. 50)

CHAPTER FOUR

Communicating Our Feelings

An experiment was conducted to determine the amount of conversation between the average husband and wife in a normal week. The participants wore portable electronic microphones that measured every word spoken from "Hi, I'm home" to "Turn up the heat—the house is cold." How much time would you guess the average couple spent talking to (or at) each other? An hour a day? No, not seven hours a week, not even one hour, or thirty minutes. Would you believe the average communication time was seventeen minutes a week?[1]

What has happened to our communication in marriage? Certainly none of us got married and then took a vow of silence. What makes us stop talking to the one we chose to spend the rest of our lives with? One husband confided in a Marriage Alive Workshop, "I can talk to my dog—but not to my wife. I always know how my dog is going to respond—he constantly loves me, so I can tell him everything. My wife's a different story—I never know how she will react."

How did the wife feel? "He pats the dog and walks right by me." She added, "I feel closed out of his life; I feel helpless." She wasn't even getting her seventeen minutes of conversation.

Four Styles of Communication

This couple needed to understand the four styles of communication that we all use at one time or another—and to use them effectively.[2]

Style One: Chit-Chat

Chit-chat refers to the surface conversations we talked about before. The "Hi, how are you's" are part of healthy communication. The problem arises when all we ever do is chit-chat. It is safe and no one is hurt, but it's shallow. Nevertheless, it is one way we all communicate.

Style Two: Attacking

Our friend, Dr. David Mace, referred to attacking as "The communication style with the sting in the tail!" We all know how that hurts. Usually when we use Style Two, we use "you" statements and ask "why" questions, like "Why did you do that?" We attack the other person without even thinking about what we're doing. Our goal when we get into Style Two (and we all will get there from time to time) is to get out of it as quickly as we can! One way to do this is simply to say, "My, that sounded like Style Two Communication to me!" This alerts the other that whether it was intended or not, you felt attacked. A wise marriage team member will accept this reminder and back off!

Once we have identified any Style Two Communication and have also identified the issue or problem to be resolved, we need to move on to Style Three Communication, the problem-solving style.

Style Three: Problem Solving

Style Three Communication is logical, problem-solving communication. The first step is to write down the problem and each person's contribution to it. Next, brainstorm possible solutions. Then choose the one that seems most appropriate and give it a try. If it doesn't work, try another possible solution. Sound simple? It is simply impossible!

When our emotions are stirred up, it's hard, if not impossible, to switch to a logical, problem-solving mode of communication. We have only seen it work on paper, never in real life! We find that at times it's like handling a hot potato—we need to back off and let it cool enough to handle. It's wise to choose a time and place to pick it up and work toward a resolution. Chapter 9, "Getting Back On When You Jump Track," will help you become proficient in using Style Three Communication. But before we can solve the problem, we need to use Style Four communication.

Style Four: Expressing Feelings

We would like to suggest a simple formula for expressing your feelings to your mate. We have used it for many years with each other, our children, and others. It is clear, simple, and nonthreatening when used with the right attitude.

"Let Me Tell You How I Feel."[3] The first part of the formula is to state clearly, directly, and in love, "Let me tell you how I feel." I feel . . . (fill in with how you feel—happy, joyful, angry, hurt, disappointed, frustrated, resentful, anxious). Express your inward feelings and emotions, and avoid attacking the other person. Don't confuse "I feel" with "I think." If you can substitute "I think" for "I feel," then it is not a feeling. For instance, "I feel that you hurt me!" expresses a thought and judgment. It is attacking, Style Two Communication in disguise. It would be much better to direct the statement toward yourself and say, "I feel hurt when this happens." You can also state your feelings by using the words "I am," as in "I am hurt."

Gary Smalley recommends painting a picture that will help your mate understand your feelings. For instance, "Honey, remember when you worked so long and hard on that proposal and took it in to your boss, only to have him toss it aside and ignore what you had carefully prepared? Well, that's how I felt when I worked so hard researching possibilities for our vacation and you didn't want to talk about it. . . ." Bam! Your mate is reliving a feeling he or she has experienced and can now identify with your feeling.

Remember, you want to express inward feelings and emotions that reflect back on you and avoid attacking the other person. It may help to realize that feelings are neither right nor wrong; they simply are there. It is also valuable to know how your mate feels.

"Now Tell Me How You Feel." After you have stated clearly and in love how you feel, ask, "Now tell me how you feel." Then be prepared to listen. Don't judge feelings. Remember they are neither right nor wrong! "Wait a minute," interrupted one husband at a workshop we were leading. "How can you say feelings are neither right nor wrong? Some feelings are just plain sinful!" This started a great discussion on the difference between how we feel and how we act (and between a thought and a true feeling). "For example," he continued, "anyone can easily get off the hook by saying, 'I don't *feel* like going to work,' 'I don't *feel* like being a thoughtful spouse,' or 'I *feel* like having an affair.'"

Before we could respond, another participant spoke up: "We may feel a certain way, but that's not an excuse for doing or not doing what is right. I wouldn't have my job very long if I told my boss, 'I don't feel like coming to work today.'"

Another picked up the discussion: "I agree, but maybe the statement, 'I don't feel like going to work' is not the real feeling or issue. Maybe you really feel worn out, taken advantage of, or bored with the job."

"Or," said another, "maybe the statement 'I feel like having an affair' is really saying on a deeper level, 'I'm bored with my marriage. I feel disconnected from my mate. I want more romance and excitement.'"

Now we were getting down to expressing feelings. Feelings are fragile, and we must handle them with care. But if we can get the real issue out on the table by sharing our feelings, we can attack the real problem (and not each other) and strengthen our own marriage team.

The couples in that workshop were beginning to get the picture when another participant spoke out: "This all sounds great, but I couldn't say how I felt if I wanted to—I just don't have a feelings vocabulary! My father only said three words, and none had anything to do with how he felt, and me, well, I'm a chip off the old block."

Remember the feelings/facts continuum from the last chapter? The feelings-oriented mate has an easier time learning to express feelings. The facts-oriented mate has feelings too but isn't comfortable in expressing them. Others might not know what they feel and need some time to think about it.

To help our group venture out into the world of feelings, we decided to come up with a list of feelings words. If you, like some of our Marriage Alive participants, have difficulty with expressing feelings, maybe our list will help you get started.

I FEEL

hurt	angry
frustrated	happy
threatened	lonely

confused

stressed

depressed

excited

proud

joyful

peaceful

energetic

sad

content

responsible

encouraged

left out

sick

trapped

squelched

betrayed

relaxed

grateful

scared

misunderstood

pressure

afraid

pessimistic

crushed

bored

ignored

uneasy

embarrassed

inspired

loved

confident

anxious

belittled

used

attacked

irritated

helpless

enlightened

overwhelmed

remorseful

broke

envious

stifled

tense

nervous

silly

abused

perplexed

alone

burdened

optimistic

enthusiastic

numb

not taken seriously

pleased

deprived

It's your turn now to communicate your feelings. Begin by evaluating how well you are communicating, and then we'll give you some suggestions for deepening your communication level.

AREAS WE TALK ABOUT

First write down areas that you can talk about and usually agree (like faith in God, common values, long-term goals, and children).

Areas we talk about and agree on are:

1. _____

2. _____

3. _____

Next list areas that you can talk about but you usually don't agree (like exercise, dieting, finances, schedules, child discipline, free time).

Areas we talk about and don't agree on are:

1. _____

2. _____

3. _____

Last list areas that you don't agree on and don't talk about (like relationships with in-laws, sexual relationship, finances, or fishing). Simply list them. Do not attempt to discuss them at this point. You don't even have to agree on your lists.

Areas we don't agree on and don't talk about are:

1. _____

2. _____

3. _____

Compare your lists. We are not striving for agreement or resolution but simply to identify these three levels of agreement or disagreement.

COMMUNICATING OUR FEELINGS

Now look at the second list, "Areas we can talk about but don't agree." Choose one of these areas. We suggest you select the lightest issue in the lot and write it down.

One area we can talk about but don't agree on is

_____

_____

Using the feelings formula, write out how you feel about this one area. (For example, "I feel anxious and fearful when we overuse our credit cards.")

I feel _____

_____

_____

_____

Now share your feelings statement with your mate and seek to understand how the other person really feels about this issue. Remember, the overused credit cards and whatever financial issue has caused it are the issues you want to attack. Do not attack each other!

We are given excellent advice in James 1:19, when we are told to be quick to listen, slow to speak, and slow to become angry. Too often we get it backward—we are slow to listen and very quick to speak and become angry. But since God gave us two ears and one mouth, maybe we are supposed to listen twice as much as we talk.

Finally we need to be aware of the total message we are sending.

Listen for the Total Message

It is not enough just to hear the words the other is saying. We need to listen for the total message. A few years ago Kodak did a study to determine what makes up "the total message" in communication. These are the results:

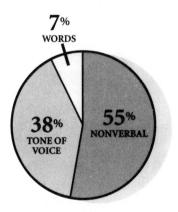

1. Our nonverbal communication accounts for 55 percent of the total message. This includes the shrugs, stares, and glares. We all know "the look!" Or the lack of any inter-

est at all. Picture one mate trying to talk as the other appears glued to the television or paper. Have you ever agreed with your mate but given another message in the disgust on your face? There is no colder place to be than with a couple who are using the right words to gloss over bitterness, hostility, and a totally different message.

2. Tone of voice accounts for 38 percent of the total message. This includes the sighs and nagging tones that creep into our conversations. Have you ever said okay when it really wasn't okay? Your tone of voice can completely reverse the message.

3. The words actually spoken make up only 7 percent of the total message.

Next time you talk to your mate, be aware of your total message—the physical response and the tone of your voice. Some changes may be in order.

Too Hard?

One workshop participant claimed, "It's just too hard. I've been me for fifty years, and I'm not going to change now. Besides, this seems fakey and unnatural to me." Maybe you feel this way too.

When we first discovered how to share our feelings, it wasn't easy for us either. It's not easy to let that other person know how we really feel. Just how will he or she use that information? When we started using the feelings formula, it was easier for Claudia than for Dave. When Claudia said how she felt, Dave would counter with, "Why do you feel that way?" or, "No one in their right mind should feel that way!" Remember that feelings are neither right nor wrong, but knowing how your mate feels is vital to communicating on a meaningful level.

Sometimes couples tell us, "We'd like to come to your workshop, but we don't want to mess with our marriage." Growing in our relationships, growing in intimacy is risky business, but the rewards of an enriched, on-track marriage are worth it. Each day we can choose to grow in our marriage, or we can choose to let things slide. We never get to the end of the track; we never arrive with perfect marriages; we never always "say it right!" For instance, we remember using all four styles of communication in one day, which shows we are in the "still growing and need improvement" category.

The Strawberry Patch

It was one of the two Saturdays each year that Dave lavishes his attention on our otherwise neglected yard. To say Dave does not enjoy yard work is an understatement. But once or twice a year he gets out there and gives it his 200 percent. This was one of those days. At breakfast as we discussed the day, we used Style One, chit-chat. Claudia spent the day lying low in the office. (She didn't want to sidetrack the gardener and had a writing deadline to meet.) Both of us felt good about the day as we were both being productive.

Late that afternoon, Dave dragged into the house—dirty, tired, sore muscles, and all—but he had "done the yard!" and wanted to show off his accomplishments. So together we went outside to take a yard tour.

Everything looked transformed and really great! Claudia was thrilled (as were our neighbors) until she came around the house to the strawberry patch. This was the year the strawberries were really going to produce, and she could already envision strawberries on ice cream, strawberries on cereal, and strawberry shortcake!

As she looked at what was supposed to be her strawberry patch, she exploded in Style Two Communication: "Why did you do that?" Dave had inadvertently pulled up all the cultivated plants and had left the wild strawberry plants that needed removing! "Dave, you've ruined my strawberries! How could you do that to me—after the hours of work

I've put in! I can't believe you didn't at least ask what to pull!" Claudia's anger was vented, and Dave secretly wished he had cemented the whole yard. Style Two was alive and well. How could we get out of this mess? After all, we wrote the book on communicating our feelings and resolving honest conflict.

We knew we couldn't solve the problem (and use Style Three) until we calmed down and got back on the same team. Both of us had said things we regretted. It was time for damage control! "Dave," Claudia began, "I didn't mean to attack you. I just feel so disappointed that my strawberries are gone. I worked hard on them, and this is so frustrating to me!"

Dave responded, "I feel frustrated too. I spent the whole day in the yard, my body hurts, I'm tired, and now I find out I did it wrong. It's just that the wild strawberries actually had little red berries on them. I assumed they were real strawberries! I'm really sorry!"

Slowly, we were beginning to calm down and Style Four Communication was helping us do it. About that time we eyed the strawberry victims. The cultured plants were in a heap in the driveway. They were the problem, and we began to focus on them. As we began to think logically, we decided to try to replant them. Clearing out the wild plants gave us more room to replant the real strawberries. Before dark, Claudia's strawberries were replanted, our relationship was restored, and we were back on the same team. Plus the strawberries lived. The next year, Dave pruned the blackberries—that's a story for another book! It takes determination and effort and courage to communicate our feelings. But take it from us, it's worth it.

TRACKING TOGETHER

Communicating Our Feelings

Purpose:
> To learn how to listen and communicate my feelings
>   to my mate
> To learn to attack the problem instead of my mate

Preparation:
> Review Chapter 4: "Communicating Our Feelings"
> Fill out exercises and be ready to discuss

Our Tracking Time is:
> Date and Time _____
> Location _____

What needs to be done to make it happen:
> 1. _____
> 2. _____
> 3. _____

Tracking-together Time:
> Together discuss the following exercises:
> 1. Areas We Talk About (p. 63)
> 2. Communicating Our Feelings (p. 64)

CHAPTER FIVE

Communicating the Positive

We'll never forget the knock on our door late one winter night when we were living in Vienna, Austria. We answered the door and were surprised and relieved to see our dear friends from Warsaw, Poland! A few days before, Poland had declared martial law. All the reports we heard indicated much tension and unrest in the country, and we were concerned about our friends. Seeing them and their three small children was a reason to celebrate.

We were doubly glad to have them safely in Vienna as they told us their story. As Karen and Tom left Warsaw, they passed tanks rumbling in. Pulling a small trailer, they brought as much with them as they could. Their immediate future was unclear.

Imagine being uprooted from your home and friends— not knowing when you might get to return—if ever! Add three small children, sickness, and other pressures. It wasn't long until our friends were about bankrupt emotionally. They needed time to think things through and regroup. We encouraged them to go away for a few days without their children.

Things looked bleak as they drove away that morning.

Karen was especially tired and depressed and even felt a little guilty about leaving their three small children. After about an hour they stopped for lunch, and for the next thirty minutes Tom told her all the things he appreciated and admired about her. He didn't just list three or four things—it was more like thirty! The way she was always there for him, her sense of humor, her sensitivity to the children's needs, her vital faith in God, her pioneer spirit (they had been living in Eastern Europe in the early eighties before the wall came down). Small things, big things, insignificant things—on and on he went, describing what he appreciated about her and her love for him. What a significant difference this thirty minutes made in her outlook on life!

Later Tom and Karen told us about their "lunch break" and the difference that time of praise had made in their whole week. From the beginning of the week Karen knew that she was loved, admired, and respected. Karen's note to us during their week together gave us a hint: "It's amazing how things come into focus when we take the time to be alone and encourage one another. We've had so much fun, but now we're ready to come home even though we still must face unsolved problems and an uncertain future." They were able to return to their home in Warsaw, and the next year we led a Marriage Alive Workshop for them in Warsaw. (We're pioneers too!)

The Other Side of the Coin

The results could have been quite different if Tom had said, "Honey, you've just got to get control of yourself. Can't you stop crying? You're not coping well at all—this just isn't like you. Your attitude is having a negative effect on our children and even on me! You're a Christian; if you tried harder, I know you could control your emotions." The week would have been a first-class disaster, and Karen would have been even more depressed. To tear down your mate is one of the most cruel and unloving things you can do—it attacks the very core of the marriage relationship.

Four to One for Praise

Psychologists tell us it takes four positive statements to offset one negative statement. Too often in marriage, the ratio of positive statements to negative statements is one to four, not four to one. What would your ratio be?

TRACKING YOUR POSITIVE/NEGATIVE TALK

Here is a personal exercise for the brave: For the next twenty-four hours, keep track of the number of positive things and the number of negative things you say to your mate. Remember four to one is just staying even. We have seen suggestions from counselors that seven to one is a more healthy ratio.

We desperately need to be encouraged by our mates. If we don't do it for each other, who will? Our bosses and co-workers? Don't count on it! Our children and teenagers? You've got to be kidding! How many children walk in and say, "Mom and Dad, I want to express my appreciation to you for your consistent discipline and for refusing to let me do certain things I want to do because you know they are not in my best interest." (Ours never did!)

Will our friends build us up? If we're fortunate they might, but we can't count on it. Our mates need our encouragement! You can be the most positive reinforcing agent in your mate's life if you choose to build up your mate instead of tearing him or her down. But how does one begin? Let us give you two tips to get you started: Push the positive and be a praiser.

Pushing the Positive

Our first suggestion is to concentrate on each other's strengths. The exercises in Chapter 3 should have already helped you to get started. It is work and does not come naturally. Look at the box below.

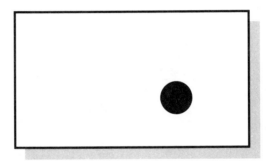

Where did your eyes immediately focus? On the small, dark spot? We tend to ignore all the light areas and see only the dark spot. In the same way, we have a tendency to concentrate on our mate's faults and on his or her weak areas. Why? Could it be that our own insecurities are showing? It's hard to build up the other person if we feel insecure ourselves. (If you are wrestling with personal problems, one of the most healthy things you can do to enrich your marriage is to get help for yourself. Today there are many excellent pastors, counselors and psychologists who, on a short-term basis, can help you personally get back on track.)

All of us have both strengths and weaknesses. Strengths and weaknesses assure us neither of success nor of failure in marriage. They are merely the setting or the field on which we play our marriage game. Remember our challenge to let each other operate out of our areas of strength. When we choose not to be threatened by our mate's strengths, even in areas where we are weak, we learn from each other. Let's look at some practical examples. Consider the following—what would be your response?

1. Your mate is a stickler for organization and you coined the statement, "Creative people are not neat." Check how you might respond.

___ ___ Not even try to be organized because you don't want to compete and lose.

___ ___ Criticize him or her for being too organized.

___ ___ Appreciate his or her gift of organization, verbally express that appreciation, and try to learn from your mate in this area.

2. You love being a hermit, but your mate is a gifted conversationalist. How do you respond?

___ ___ Criticize your mate for being too talkative.

___ ___ Send your mate as your representative to all social functions.

____ ____ Appreciate his or her natural talent in this area, verbalize your appreciation, and benefit from your mate's insights.

Every day we make choices to benefit from our mate's strengths or to be threatened by them. Let us encourage you to appreciate the strengths your mate brings to your team. Remember we want cooperation not competition!

The Arps are among that species in the Western world known as "tennis buffs." That doesn't mean we are super players, but we have managed to win a few matches. Sometimes we even win when our opponents are more skilled than we are. Bob and Marie individually are much better tennis players than we are, but when we play doubles together, we usually win because Bob and Marie have never learned to play together as a team. They put each other down as if they are competing with each other. In essence, they are two people playing singles on the same side of the net.

Although we make our share of blunders, we minimize our errors through teamwork. We've studied our strengths and weaknesses and know when we need to play at the net or play back. We've spent time working out our strategy. We don't always win, but when we lose we're still pulling together (except on those days we get derailed). But most of the time we enjoy teaming up for tennis.

In many ways marriage is like playing doubles in tennis. Teaming up can lead to positive growth. We want to be partners instead of opponents. This involves being willing to build a partnership. There certainly is no place in marriage for competition, but there is much room for building up our mates.

Some of our closest times have been when things were rough on the outside. Before we began to work full time in the area of marriage and family enrichment, we went through a long, hard year, which included many meetings, proposals, deadlines, and delays. Many times we were weary and ready to give up. For each two steps forward, it seemed there were three steps back! I don't think we would have made it if we had not been on each other's team, willing to encourage the other when we were down. We also benefited from each other's individual strengths. Claudia's creativity and organizational ability helped us get our proposal formulated. Dave's enthusiasm helped promote it. Claudia's discipline and drive kept it going, but when she became discouraged, Dave's slow, methodical consistency gave stability and helped us hang in until we got the "go-ahead." Alone, either of us would have given up.

Does your mate know you're glad he or she is on your team? When have you told him or her so? If it hasn't been in the last week, get busy!

Be a Praiser

The word *praise* comes from a Latin word for worth, indicating a vital connection between the two. Webster defines praise as "to commend the worth of; to glorify God." Let us add our own definition of praise:

1. Praise Is Describing What You Appreciate About Your Mate

Here are some practical tips for praising one another:

Be Specific. Examples:
"I appreciate your initiative and creativity in our sexual relationship."
"I appreciate your thoughtfulness in calling me when you're going to be late."
"I like the way you listen to me when I try to express my inner feelings."

Let us add a note of caution. If you are specific and personal in your praise, make sure your mate receives it personally. For instance, if you send a personal letter to your mate at work, mark the envelope "Personal." Three businessmen still think the Arps are a little strange. Dave tells the story:

"I had just gotten a new answering machine in my office. Immediately after hooking it up, I left to meet three men for lunch. We still had business to conduct, so we all returned to my office. I was delighted to see the red light blinking on my brand new answering machine. Imagine my shock, to hear a very intimate message from Claudia—the only problem was, I didn't know how to turn off the machine, and to this day those three men aren't sure it was my wife! (By the way, as soon as we finished our business, I closed up shop and rushed home!)"

Describe—don't compare. Examples:
Wrong: "You are the best kisser in the whole world!"
(How would you know?)
Right: "I like the way you kiss me."

2. Praise Is Affirming What Your Mate Is Becoming

Goethe, the great German poet and philosopher, said, "If you treat a man as he is, he will stay as he is. If you treat him as if he were what he ought to be and could be, he will become that bigger and better man." Begin to look at your mate through Goethe's eyes. Jesus demonstrated this when He looked at impulsive Peter and called him a rock!

One participant in a Marriage Alive Workshop confided, "I've been in the habit of focusing on the negative instead of the positive—it's so much easier! I just seem to forget the positive growing edges of my mate and instead put my mind on the weak areas. I'm beginning to realize that all relationships are fluid and never stand still. I want our marriage to move forward and grow. Starting right this moment I'm going to commit myself to look at my mate through Goethe's eyes and every day find something to affirm!"

Why not make that same commitment? Take a few minutes right now to list the growing edges of your mate's life. For instance, is your mate in the process of taking a risk right now? Perhaps learning a new skill or even making a career change? If you can't think of anything to write down on this list, pray and ask God to reveal to you potential growing edges in your mate's life.

GROWING EDGES TO AFFIRM

The growing edges in my mate's life (as I see them) are:

1. _____
2. _____
3. _____

The growing edges in my life (as I see them) are:

1. _____
2. _____
3. _____

3. Praise Is Sincere

Flattery is not praise. Flattery is insincere and makes the recipient feel uncomfortable and manipulated. Flattery is counterfeit praise.

It's fun to get an honest compliment; if we have worked hard to improve in an area, it's great to have a spouse notice. For the last year Claudia, motivated by a back injury, has worked faithfully on physical fitness. Out of character as it may be, she lifts weights, exercises, and walks fifteen-minute miles. While her major motivation is to have a healthy back, the side benefits include better muscle tone, less flab, and lower numbers on the bathroom scales. As Dave began to notice these changes, Claudia appreciated his positive comments: "Hey, you look slim in those slacks" or "That skirt is too big. Why not go shopping and splurge on a new outfit?" She's glad he was sincere about that last comment, and she immediately took him up on the suggestion. She was also glad he didn't use flattery and suggest she get a bikini—that thin she's not, and varicose veins don't just go away!

4. Praise Is Verbal

We can have all kinds of nice thoughts about our mates, but power is only released when they are verbalized. How much praise power have you released today? Perhaps you have no positive thoughts to release. Negative talk is usually preceded by negative thoughts.

Philippians 4:8 gives us the solution for this dilemma: "Finally, brethren, whatever things are true . . . noble . . . just . . . pure . . . lovely . . . of good report, if there is any virtue and if there is anything praiseworthy—meditate on these things."

Too often we do the opposite. Whatever is untrue, whatever is wrong or negative, those are the things we tend to dwell on.

Positive thoughts are worth developing. However, stable habits take time and persistence to develop, so be prepared to persevere! One way to begin is to make your own Philippians 4:8 list.

MAKING A PHILIPPIANS TREASURE LIST

Think about your mate and list one thing in the following categories.

1. One thing that is true (like, your love and commitment to me):

   _____

   _____

   _____

2. One thing that is honorable (like, your honesty and integrity in business and financial affairs):

   _____

   _____

   _____

3. One thing about my mate that is right (like, you make time for us to work on our marriage goals):

   _____

   _____

   _____

4. One thing that is pure (like, you are faithful to me):

_____

_____

_____

5. One thing that is lovely (like, I like your being a creative lover):

_____

_____

_____

6. One thing that is of good report (like, you willingly volunteer your time to help make our community a better place to live):

_____

_____

_____

When you feel yourself moving into a negative thinking pattern, pull out your list and dwell on your mate's positive qualities.

A group of couples in a Marriage Alive Growth Group were studying how to encourage their mates. Most admitted that they had not developed the habit of praise. They committed themselves to giving their mates five compliments during the next week. One mate confided to us at the end of the week, "It felt so strange to hear words of encouragement and praise come out of my lips."

Think about today or yesterday. How many times did you criticize your mate? How many times did you praise your mate? Remember that praise is verbal, and then consider these ways to get with it!

Use Written Praise. Don't overlook written praise. Consider the following:

a. Notes and jingles
b. Letters and cards
c. Acrostics

One Thanksgiving Claudia did an acrostic for Dave and for each of our children. Dave's read:

Dave is . . .
Truthful
Helpful
Athletic
Nice
Kind
Super
Great Dad
Intelligent
Very creative lover
Interesting
Never a bore
God's good gift to me!

You can get a good buy on Valentine cards on February 15. One year we stocked up and then kept hiding them. When either one of us found one, we recycled it and hid it for the other to find. We kept them going for months.

Make a list of things you appreciate about your mate. One clever husband made a list of thirty-one things he appreciated about his wife. He typed them, cut them up, folded them, put them in capsules, and gave them to his wife with the following prescription: "Take one a day for a month." *Give coupons*. Include things like:

1. Free—one back rub with hot oil
2. Breakfast in bed
3. Dinner for two at your favorite restaurant
4. A five-mile hike together.

Give a gift for no reason at all. Once, on a special promotional offer from a local department store, Dave was able to purchase a number of small bottles of perfume and samples of lotions. He individually wrapped each one, and each evening he hid one under Claudia's pillow. The first night, she was surprised, the second night even more surprised, and the third and fourth nights, she got in the hang of it and started going to bed even earlier.

A word of caution . . . If your mate reads this chapter and you begin to get little gifts, cards, and extra attention, please don't say, "I know—it's just because you read *The Marriage Track!*" Please express your thanks and appreciation in your own creative way and say a big "Thank you" to God for such a thoughtful mate!

Finally, try to laugh together.

Develop a Sense of Humor

A first cousin of encouragement is laughter. Being able to laugh together definitely adds an element of fun. When we're on a positive track together, it's just easier to laugh, and when we are able to laugh together, we seem to stay more positive with each other. When we're under stress, we benefit from looking and trying to find some way to lighten things up.

We know one young couple who are experts. The pressures of law school, work, and other responsibilities were taking their toll, like caring for their three cats. Many couples share with us the fun of pet ownership and how pets can relieve tension, but imagine the wife's surprise when she walked into their modest apartment after a stressful day at work to find all three cats wearing ties!

We all have difficult situations in our lives. If we can step back, not take ourselves so seriously, and find something to laugh about, as this couple did, we can keep our relationship on a more positive track.

As you know, we are quite different. Recently Claudia was telling Dave about all the pressure and stress she was feeling and how she has spent a couple of hours wide awake in the middle of the night worrying about it all. Dave's comment? "If one worried in the middle of the night, just what specifically would one worry about?" Claudia, the gifted worrier in our family, found Dave's response so completely foreign to her way of thinking, it was funny.

Remember the Scripture from Ecclesiastes we talked about in Chapter 1, "If one falls down, the other can pick him up"? That's exactly what we can do for our mate if we are willing to look for the positive and the humorous. One of the fun parts of our Marriage Alive Workshop is the time couples spend writing a letter of encouragement to each other. We want you to stop right now and participate in this exercise of encouragement.

WRITING A LETTER

Simply write a letter to your mate, and describe what you appreciate about him or her. If you look back through the last few chapters to the exercises you have completed, you will find many positive things to include. Actually mail the letter to your mate. If you send it to an office address, please, oh please, remember to write personal on the envelope. (We won't tell you the story of the mate who forgot to write personal.) Stamp it and drop it in the mail. Your mate will be the proud recipient, and it just may boomerang back to you! One couple who participated in a Marriage Alive Workshop told us how excited they were when the mail carrier delivered their workshop letters. Life was extremely hectic for them at that time, so they decided not to open their letters immediately. They extended the fun and benefit of their letter-writing session to a weekend when grandparents could keep their two small children. They took off for an overnight at a quaint bed and breakfast, letters in hand.

After a romantic dinner they opened and read their letters. It set the stage for wonderful closeness. Why don't you consider doing the same? Your marriage will be the benefactor!

TRACKING TOGETHER

Communicating the Positive

Purpose:
> To learn how to build up instead of tear down my
> mate
> To learn to break the negative thought pattern by
> learning to praise

Preparation:
> Review Chapter 5, "Communicating the Positive"
> Fill out exercises and be ready to discuss

Our Tracking Time is:
> Date and time _____
> Location _____

What needs to be done to make it happen:
> 1. _____
> 2. _____
> 3. _____

Tracking-together Time:
> Together discuss the following exercises:
> 1. Growing Edges to Affirm (p. 78)
> 2. Making a Philippians Treasure List (p. 80)
> 3. Writing a Letter (p. 84)

CHAPTER SIX

Setting Goals for Your Marriage

I'm comfortable setting goals for our company," said a recent Marriage Alive participant. Ralph was the vice president of a major corporation and had gotten where he was by setting goals and then working hard to achieve them. "But," he continued, "I've never considered setting goals with my wife for our marriage. It makes sense. How have we survived twenty-five years without it? What should we do first—I feel like a real novice. Is it too late?"

We were happy to tell Ralph and Norma that it wasn't too late and that the next session in our workshop would help them to set marriage goals. We are also happy to tell you that wherever you are in your marriage—newlyweds or long-time partners—it's not too late to set goals for the future.

Maybe you've heard the adage "You can't teach an old dog new tricks!" That may be true of dogs, but a recent study of the aged shows that we can change our behavior until the day we die. We are never too old to learn or to work at improving our relationship with our mate—or to set marriage goals!

It can work for you just as it did for Ralph and Norma.

You wouldn't be in Chapter 6 of this book if you weren't serious about improving your marriage. You have a lot of good ideas, but how can you put them all together?

Sometimes it's not so much a problem of knowing what to do, but doing what we know. Remember it takes three weeks to make a new habit and six weeks to feel good about it. In this chapter we want to help you work out your own plan of attack, and as you continue in *The Marriage Track,* you'll be in the process of developing the habit of having an intentional marriage, a high-priority marriage. Your tracks will be headed in the same direction and you will actually be going somewhere!

What Were Your Expectations?

To set valid goals for your marriage, you need to look at the expectations you had when you said, "I do." We take this kind of a step back at our Marriage Alive Workshops when we ask couples to share why they chose to invest their weekend in this way. Sometimes we get unexpected answers, like the one from a couple who came because babysitting was offered or from the couple who thought the weekend was tax deductible! But the Harrisons, a couple in their sixties, had another reason. They had paid the registration for their son and daughter-in-law. At the last minute the younger couple couldn't attend and the Harrisons didn't want to lose their investment, so they came instead.

Mr. Harrison seemed very uncomfortable, and when they had an opportunity to discuss the first exercise with each other—well, it was very quiet in their corner. As the workshop progressed, they began to relax, and by the end of the weekend, they were strong advocates of marriage enrichment. Since that workshop, we keep running into people who know the Harrisons and we appreciate the free advertisement. They're recommending it to all their older friends!

It's easier to adjust our expectations when, like the Harrisons, we start with few and are surprised at how great something is. In marriage, it seems to work the other way. Often we come into marriage with stars in our eyes and a belief that our future mate is going to meet all our needs and expectations. When the honeymoon is over, our hormones have settled down, and we get in the everyday rut, marriage may not be quite what we expected.

Then, too, our expectations may not have been the same. Recently a group of teenagers were questioned about what they wanted in a mate when they married. One boy said he wanted an "old-fashioned" wife just like his mom, one who would find cleaning the house, cooking, washing, and ironing his clothes to be creative and exciting. One girl in the same group said she wanted to have an exciting career as well as five children, and she was sure that she and her husband would share home responsibilities fifty-fifty. We looked at each other and thought—if these two get together, they're going to need more than our book and workshop!

What were your expectations before marriage? Listen to what others have said:

- The main reason I got married was for sex.
- I expected my mate to meet my needs—to be a lot like me.
- What I wanted in marriage was romance!
- I was looking for security and love, someone I could trust and lean on.
- What was really important to me in my marriage was to have peace and harmony, to know that when we went to bed at night everything was okay.

Obviously, some of these couples were in for some shocks when their mates were unable to live up to their expectations. Dr. Selma Miller, past president of the Association of Marriage and Family Counselors, states: "The most common cause of marriage problems is that partners' needs are in conflict, but they can't discuss the conflict because they don't know one exists. They only know they are miserable."[1]

What Are Your Expectations?

Do you desire intimacy, closeness, and deep sharing of life's experiences with your mate? Sharing life deeply with one another and being loved, trusted, and appreciated even when the other understands our weaknesses gives us a sense of identity and self-confidence in our marriage relationship.

Let's look at seven areas of expectations in marriage. As you read through the list, rank these expectations in order of their importance to you (1 is highest; 7, lowest). Then go back through the list and rank them according to how you think your mate sees them.[2]

UNDERSTANDING OUR EXPECTATIONS

__ __ 1. Security—the knowledge of permanence in the relationship and of financial and material well-being

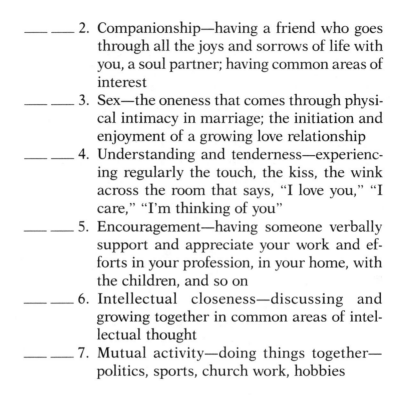

___ ___ 2. Companionship—having a friend who goes through all the joys and sorrows of life with you, a soul partner; having common areas of interest

___ ___ 3. Sex—the oneness that comes through physical intimacy in marriage; the initiation and enjoyment of a growing love relationship

___ ___ 4. Understanding and tenderness—experiencing regularly the touch, the kiss, the wink across the room that says, "I love you," "I care," "I'm thinking of you"

___ ___ 5. Encouragement—having someone verbally support and appreciate your work and efforts in your profession, in your home, with the children, and so on

___ ___ 6. Intellectual closeness—discussing and growing together in common areas of intellectual thought

___ ___ 7. Mutual activity—doing things together—politics, sports, church work, hobbies

Share your rankings with one another. Then look back at the list and circle the expectations that may not have been met. Think about these as you set goals for your marriage.

Tracking Your Goals

How can you set goals for your marriage? We do this by considering the following three questions:

1. How far apart are your expectations?
2. Where do you want to be—what style of marriage do you want? (Have you identified some expectations that you'd like to meet?)
3. How can you devise a plan of action to get where you want to be?

How Far Apart Are You?

The loudspeaker of the big jet clicked on, and the captain's voice announced: "Now there's no cause for alarm, but we thought you passengers should be informed that for the last two hours, we've been flying without the benefit of radio, compass, radar, or navigational beam. This means, in the broadest sense of the word, that we're not sure in which direction we are heading. On the brighter side of the picture, however, I'm sure you'll be interested to know that we're making excellent time!"

We can imagine your response to such an announcement. Yet many of our marriages are set on such a course. We don't just want to be making good time; we should know where we are going. Some couples discover that they are drifting in their marriage, but they are afraid to rock the boat. Then something comes along and jolts them anyway.

Where are you in your marriage today? To help determine where you are today, compare your relationship to the marriage involvement chart below.[3]

MINIMUM   MODERATE   MAXIMUM

Degrees of Involvement in Marriage

Minimum Involvement

In a minimum involvement marriage, the lives of the husband and wife overlap very little. They go different directions and meet only occasionally. They have separate interests and hobbies and are usually quite independent of each other.

"I keep forgetting my husband is out of town," said an acquaintance of ours who has this style of marriage. We used to question the stability of their marriage, wondering why they did not experience more tension since they spent very little time together. For us, that sort of distance would be uncomfortable, but it was working for them.

Maximum Involvement

We have chosen a maximum involvement marriage style; our lives are deeply involved with each other. We do seminars together; we write together; we enjoy spending time with each other. We make most decisions together and share our innermost thoughts and dreams.

Our circles overlap to a great extent, although we still have interests and activities that do not include the other. Actually we have to work on having a little separateness in our marriage. It's easy to be together "too much."

You can see why we question our friends who have chosen minimum involvement. But if both partners agree about the amount of involvement, then we should not consider their marriage rocky.

Moderate Involvement

Most couples tend to fall in the moderate involvement category. Mike and Dianne work hard at keeping their circles overlapping at a moderate level. They are friends and lovers but also try to manage separate careers.

Mike is a talented young graphic artist and is definitely on his way up. When the opportunity to go into business for himself came along, he and Dianne spent many days and hours talking through the implications for their marriage and family—they have two young children. They decided to go for it.

Mike's hours are long, and most weekends he has to finish an urgent project "yesterday." Dianne's job is not so stressful, though, and neither has a job that requires travel.

Still it's a real challenge to make their circles overlap at all! Rather than complain, they look for ways to work together to accomplish household projects. For instance, it wouldn't be fun for us, but together they painted the outside of their house. They put up a fence in the back yard so that their kids could play safely and designed a rock garden that makes us jealous!

For Mike and Dianne, it's hard work to stay in the moderate involvement zone. The maximum level is just not realistic for them, and the minimum level is below their expectations for their marriage.

All three marriage styles can be workable. And in between these three styles is a wide range of varying shades and degrees of involvement. Where would you place your marriage? After working through these six chapters, are you closer to each other? Do your circles overlap more or less? Are you in agreement about the amount of mutual involvement you both desire for your marriage?

THINGS WE DO TOGETHER AND APART

Take time right now to make the two lists suggested below and to discuss how much your circles overlap.

Things we do together:

1. _____

2. _____

3. _____

4. _____

5. _____

Things we do apart from each other:

1. _____

2. _____

3. _____

4. _____

5. _____

Think back to the expectations you had when you said, "I do." If mutual activity—doing things together—was high on your list, do your activities reflect that involvement? If companionship—having a friend who goes through all the joys and sorrows of life—was a high priority, does your relationship reflect that kind of friendship? How about individual closeness or understanding and tenderness? If your answer is "No," don't give up. Many couples have realized how different their marriage was from their expectations and have been able to make a mid-course adjustment by answering the question "Where do you want to be?"

Where Do You Want to Be?

The next step is to discuss together the degree of involvement you both desire. Compromise will be part of the process. Pull out your list of feelings words from pages 61–62 and use Style Four Communication—expressing how you feel and not attacking the other—as you talk through this question.

How involved do you want to be in each other's lives? Would you choose Diagram A, B, or C?

THINGS WE WANT TO DO

Things we would like to do together:

1. _____
2. _____
3. _____
4. _____

Things we would like to start doing separately:

1. _____
2. _____
3. _____

Our challenge to you is to find what works for you! Realistically, how much mutual time do you have? One young doctor told us, "When I get home and we eat and get the children in bed, the only way I can stay up is to prop my eyelids open with toothpicks. (He's a morning lark.) To plan dates and try to do projects and exercises just doesn't work for us. They fall flat, and then we both get discouraged. Where do we start?"

Our answer was to start with the time they did have. The most important question is "What are you doing with the time you have?"

One couple we know make a daily practice of arising fifteen minutes early each morning. They start their day with a cup of tea and a quiet time together. They read a passage of Scripture and pray together. They share their inner thoughts and feelings with each other and start the day in touch with God and in touch with each other. When a friend asked them, "How in the world do you ever find time to do that every day?" they smiled and responded with conviction: "Oh, my goodness, we don't think of it as finding time. We have to take time. When we do this, we know we are centered."

Are you centered together? What is your focus? What are your expectations, and are they realistic?

Be Realistic

Recently at a Marriage Alive Workshop, we stayed at a lovely bed and breakfast in the North Carolina mountains. This B&B was run by a couple from Atlanta who had left the corporate world of sports cars and life in the fast lane. Visions of being a team and working together, plus the peace and serenity of the North Carolina mountains, lured them to buy this particular bed and breakfast.

Yet we never saw them together! The wife shared, "Our circles don't overlap at all. Basically we work in shifts. As a matter of fact, our circles just keep getting bigger and bigger and farther apart. We tend to go around problems, and we're missing each other completely."

It was time for this couple to sit down and regroup. Their expectations were unmet, partly because their expectations were unrealistic. Our advice to this couple was to try the fifteen-minutes-a-day time to touch base and regroup.

Obviously they needed more time together than that, but at least it's a starting point.

Setting Realistic Marriage Goals

The next step is to set realistic goals for your marriage together with your mate. Did we hear you groan? Remember Ralph wouldn't be where he was in his corporation without planning objectives and goals. Business thrives on goal setting, and marriages desperately need more of it! But few couples have ever taken the time to set specific objectives for their marriages, much less drawn up a plan to accomplish them.

A marriage goal is a target toward which you and your mate both agree to work. It's a way you intend to grow. Let us give you some examples of marriage goals:

1. To develop a deeper relationship with my mate, to develop common interests and get to know my mate better
2. To improve communication with my mate and to learn to express myself in a better way
3. To improve and become more creative in our sexual relationship
4. To become more united and responsible in our finances
5. To learn to resolve conflict in a positive way that builds our relationship instead of tearing it down
6. To choose a common project to do together or choose something to learn together or do a service project for someone else

Choose Your Goals

Take time right now to choose your own goals for your marriage. You can't work on all areas at the same time, so pick your major area for the next few weeks. We suggest starting with an easy area in which you can quickly see some progress. As you build your faith level, you can go on to more difficult areas.

SETTING MARRIAGE GOALS

Goals for our marriage (for instance, to learn to concentrate on our strengths, not our weaknesses, or to commit ourselves more deeply to building one another up and not tearing down) are:

1. _____

2. _____

3. _____

4. _____

5. _____

The first area we will work on is:

_____

_____

Once you know the type of marriage you want, the final step is to devise a plan of action to achieve your goals.

How Are You Going to Get There?

Three simple words can guide you as you devise a plan of action: What? How? When?

What is the marriage goal you have chosen? For example, you might choose "to improve communication with my mate and to learn to express myself in a better way."

How? Logically, the next thing to ask is "How am I going to reach this goal?" The answer to this question needs to be achievable and measurable so you'll know when you get there. How are you going to open up communication with your mate? What activities will help you accomplish your goal? For example:

1. For the next five weeks we will spend one evening a week and will continue through Part 2 and Part 3 of *The Marriage Track*.
2. We will plan a weekend away without the children in the next two months.
3. We will each read a book on communication and discuss it.
4. We will practice identifying our styles of communication and attempt to use Style Four as much as possible.

When? Without answering this final question, you probably will not reach your goal. This is the time to pull out your calendars and planners and write (in ink) the time for doing the above activities. If you are going to set aside Tuesday nights, then write the time on your calendar for every Tuesday night. When are you going to manage a weekend away? Pencil in several possibilities and begin working on freeing your schedule. What book on communication are you going to read? Block out time to sit down and read it. Now, commit yourselves to following your plan.

Let's look at another illustration.

What: To improve and become more creative in our sexual relationship. What can you do to deepen this part of your marriage that is measurable, achievable, and compatible with your other marriage goals?

How: Short-term plans:

1. Read a book on this subject together, such as *The Gift of Sex* by Joyce and Clifford Penner or *Intended for Pleasure* by Ed and Gaye Wheat.
2. Set aside two hours each week to be alone together for the next four weeks.
3. Plan a twenty-four-hour getaway without the children in the next six weeks.
4. Make a list of creative things you both would like to do (like give each other a back rub with warm scented oil, take a bubble bath for two, or play romantic music and light the candles).

When: Scheduling:

1. We will read together Monday and Thursday before we go to bed (Who knows where that may lead?).
2. We will arrange our schedules to be free for two hours for lunch on Friday (Kids will be at Grandma's or school or wherever—just not where we will be!).
3. We will try to take our getaway the first weekend of next month.
4. Together on Saturday we will make a list of ideas and put them in a jar to draw out at the appropriate time!

What About Interruptions?

One thing is sure—interruptions will appear. Some weeks your time together will just not happen, due to sick children, drop-in guests, or other unforseeable events. But even if you don't follow through with every single activity, you will have gone a lot further toward reaching your goal than if you had not planned at all. So be realistic, but also persevere, and you will be on the right track!

That's what Ralph and Norma had to do. During the last session of the workshop, Ralph and Norma decided to continue through *The Marriage Track*. Their goal was to do one chapter every other week. On the alternating weeks, they decided to choose one of the fun dates in Part 3.

The first week, Ralph had to go out of town unexpectedly on business. He and Norma compromised and had a ten-minute phone date. To add a little creativity and spice, they faxed love notes to each other. The second week they were all set, and unexpected company dropped in. Once again their expectations were not fulfilled. The third week they again planned their date. The cog this week was another business trip. This time Norma's schedule was clear, and they went together and took *The Marriage Track* with them. They had their date on the airplane. It was so much fun they decided that whenever they took a trip and flew they would do *The Marriage Track*.

If your life is hectic like Ralph and Norma's, take their example. You may have to be creative and flexible. So whether you have your date on a plane or train, or in a doctor's waiting room, an emergency room, or a coffee shop, spend time together. It'll help your marriage fly!

What Next?

Now that you have completed Part 1—hopefully, you've gotten your marriage on track—what's next? Part 2 is designed to help you keep your marriage on track and get back on when you accidentally jump off. You'll have the opportunity to look at some specific areas in your marriage like making your love life more creative, communicating positively while resolving honest conflict, and the secrets of having a truly Christian marriage. Be encouraged; keep tracking; your marriage journey is just beginning!

TRACKING TOGETHER

Setting Goals for Your Marriage

Purpose:
> To reexamine my expectations for marriage
> To evaluate where our marriage is and where we want it to be
> To set marriage goals and a realistic plan for achieving them

Preparation:
> Review Chapter 6, "Setting Goals for Your Marriage"
> Fill out exercises and be ready to discuss

Our Tracking Time is:
> Date and Time _____
>
> Location _____

What needs to be done to make it happen:
> 1. _____
> 2. _____
> 3. _____

Tracking-together Time:
> Together discuss the following exercises:
> 1. Understanding Our Expectations (p. 90)
> 2. Things We Do Together and Apart (p. 94)
> 3. Things We Want to Do (p. 96)
> 4. Setting Marriage Goals (p. 99)

PART TWO

STAYING ON TRACK—EVEN WHEN YOU DERAIL

CHAPTER SEVEN

Learning to Say the "S" Word (or Building a Creative Love Life)

Sex! There, we've said it. . . . We've said the "S" word. Why are people so hesitant to talk openly about the sexual dimension of life? When we stop and think about it, we realize sexual thoughts and feelings are prominent throughout our lives.

- In the teenage years, we dream about it, and if coming from a Judeo-Christian value system, we do all we can to use self-restraint.
- In the twenties and thirties as the children begin to arrive on the scene, we dream about the day we'll once again have the energy for it and fewer interruptions.
- In our forties, as our own children become teenagers, our thoughts about sex focus on our kids and on our hope that they will not experiment with it.
- In the fifties and sixties, the nest empties, and as one friend said, "By then we have forgotten how!" or, we might add, we're just too busy.
- The seventies and eighties allow time for sexual fantasies vicariously lived out through watching the soaps

on television. For many of the elderly the "S" word is again a dream.

While sexual thoughts and feelings are close to the surface during all the stages of life, why is it so hard to say the "S" word? Recently, while we were leading a class for parents whose children are entering adolescence, the "S" word came up in a discussion of sex education. Members of this group were definitely in the "worrying about our own kids" stage.

Their fears are not without foundation. Our world grossly misuses God's positive gift of sex. Sex is used to sell just about anything. After all, what does the kind of detergent we use have to do with a fulfilling sexual relationship? Does a mouthwash or toothpaste really give sex appeal?

When we were growing up, the culture applauded fidelity. Today young people are told to have "safe sex," and the media presents sex as total ecstasy with no responsibilities or consequences. No wonder the parents in our group were scared. "I don't want to tell my child about sex because I want her to remain innocent," said one concerned parent.

We were amazed at this parent's naivete. First, if this eleven-year-old didn't know about the "S" word, we would be surprised. Secondly, what attitude was this parent unintentionally passing on to her daughter? If no knowledge of sex equals innocence, does an understanding of the sexual dimension of life equal guilt? This kind of fallacious thinking is the source of some of our own inhibitions and hesitations to use the "S" word.

Think back into your own childhood with us. What were your earliest impressions of sex? Did you believe the "birds and bees" story?

One girl asked her grandmother, "Where did I come from?"

The grandmother replied, "Honey, the stork brought you."

"But what about my mommy? Where did she come from?" she continued to probe.

"We found her in the cabbage patch."

"What about you?" the granddaughter asked.

"My parents found me behind the rosebush."

The next day at school the little girl reported to her class, "There has not been a normal birth in our family for three generations!"

Claudia's earliest memory of any conversation about sex was in the third or fourth grade when an older friend told her what boys and girls do to each other to make babies. It didn't sound like fun, and at that point Claudia decided to be an old maid! Dave also got his initial impression about the "S" word from friends—just as inaccurate and confusing.

Now it's your turn to remember.

MY "SEX EDUCATION"

My first memory of talking about sex is

_____

_____

_____

_____

_____

Whether our parents used the "S" word or not, our being here is evidence our parents had at least some interest in sex. Is that hard to believe? Probably all kids at some time are convinced that their parents really "don't do it!" It's especially hard for teenagers to think about their parents as sexual creatures.

What do you remember from your home of origin? You may want to check any of the following statements that describe your childhood environment.

___ My parents never or rarely used the "S" word.

___ My parents openly talked about sex in a way that made it seem natural and positive.

___ My parents rarely showed physical affection for each other or for me.

___ I come from a family of huggers. My parents were very affectionate with each other and with me.

___ I was uncomfortable asking my parents about sexual things. I basically learned about the specifics of sex from other sources.

___ I was comfortable asking my parents about sexual things. They were my major source of sex education.

___ I received mixed messages about sex. I wasn't sure if it was good or bad.

___ Based on my parents' attitudes, I looked forward to having a sexual relationship in marriage someday.

Now evaluate what types of things you checked from the above list. If your parents were comfortable with the "S" word and were open and honest and positive about sex with you, count yourself among the very fortunate. If, more typically, your parents choked on the word *sex* and left many unasked questions unanswered, you may have entered marriage with a confused picture of sex. For instance, growing up did you hear comments like "Don't be loose" or "She's a fast girl. Don't be like her!" You weren't sure what "loose" and "fast" actually meant, but you knew they weren't positive.

Then your own hormones began to "click on." You met that special girl or boy, and sexual feelings you didn't know you could ever have began to surface. Not only did you try your darndest to use self-restraint, but you began to feel guilty for having all those feelings!

Those who grew up in conservative homes may have gotten the impression that sex is sinful. Certainly God intended the sexual union to be experienced within the framework of marriage, but the Scriptures also teach that God created sex for our enjoyment and pleasure as well as procreation. Many overlook the fact that sex was God's idea.

The Bible discusses sex openly and matter-of-factly, acknowledging that it is a precious gift from God. Consider Proverbs 5:18–19:

> Let your fountain be blessed,
> And rejoice with the wife of your youth.
> As a loving deer and a graceful doe,
> Let her breasts satisfy you at all times;
> And always be enraptured with her love.

Look again at Genesis 2:24–25: "For this cause a man shall leave his father and his mother and shall cleave to his wife, and they shall become one flesh. And they were both naked, the man and his wife, and were not ashamed" (NASB). God put His stamp of approval on the sexual union in marriage. He not only approves of it; He originated it! It is to be an expression of love between husband and wife, fulfilling and enjoyable. Why then is it so hard to say the "S" word?

Back to Our Dating Days . . .

In recalling our dating days, we have to admit that our relationship was far from platonic. We were quite familiar with each other, but did manage to save the big "S" for marriage. Even with the culture working with us, it wasn't all that easy. Once we read a book on how to handle sexual impulses. The author suggested that when we felt tempted, we should get out of the car and run around it five times. That was about as helpful as taking cold showers! Then we finally made it to that big day—our wedding day—only to discover that "doing what comes naturally just wasn't enough."

Think about it. First, you've got all these conflicting messages. For what seems like an eternity, you have been working your hardest to avoid the "big sin." Suddenly you say, "I do," and it is now God's good gift to you. It is now okay to experience the big "S." And then you begin to realize that instructions for sexual fulfillment were not included with your marriage license. Maybe, like us, you felt a little let down when you discovered that here is another learning experience in which you slowly develop expertise and new skills. For us it didn't happen instantly as it does on television. Our marital camera didn't fade into instant ecstasy!

We must admit, we got married thirty years ago, and getting any kind of counseling before marriage was still the exception. Today, premarital counseling may help, but face it—you can't learn to swim until you get into the water.

The problem with the "S" word is that we talk about it with friends and with each other before marriage, but once we say "I do," talking about sex becomes a "taboo." When things don't instantly click in the sexual arena, many conclude that sex is overrated—it's okay but not what you had hoped it would be. So you compensate in other areas of your relationship and relegate the "S" word to an inactive vocabulary file. Some cover up even with their mates: "Honey, I'm just too tired . . . too busy . . . the neighbors will hear us." Before long the sexual part of marriage is buried under your inhibitions, lack of knowledge, and boredom. Whatever happened to all those sexual feelings you had trouble controlling before marriage?

With today's statistics, we can't leave this subject without addressing those who tried using self-restraint before marriage but just didn't make it. You feel guilty and wish you could go back and wipe the slate clean. Added to the dilemma of overcoming inhibitions, boredom, and lack of knowledge, is a big hunk of guilt.

Maybe you regret that you had several previous sexual partners before you met your mate. This could have been before you embraced the Christian faith or—even more guilt producing—you may have slipped while you were trying to follow the Lord. Maybe as a child you were the victim of sexual abuse or incest or have gone through the trauma of rape.

Whatever your past, there is healing, forgiveness, and hope. While *The Marriage Track* is not adequate to deal with deep-seated problems, we encourage you to get help if your past is blocking your future. Do not hesitate to seek counseling from a qualified professional. If you don't know where to find one, begin by consulting your pastor. Help is available, but it's up to you to take the initiative to find it!

The Newlywed Game—Learning to Say the "S" Word

Let's move on to our early marriage days. Our initial disappointment became a challenge to learn and develop expertise. We decided to tackle building a fulfilling sexual relationship with all the gusto we could muster. We were still in college and as poor as church mice. Our major form of entertainment was working on our sex life. We made some basic commitments to each other that helped us to get our sexual relationship on the right track, and thirty years later we are still tracking together. Some of the discoveries we made in those first years of marriage follow.

We had to *talk* about it! We had to develop our "S" word vocabulary. How would the other know what feels good unless he or she was told? In some ways it was like learning a new language and was awkward at first. For years we had tried not even to think these thoughts, much less verbalize them! We also had to be willing to talk about our fears and inhibitions. One of us was much more inhibited than the other, so a major part of "talking it out" was the willingness of the other to listen!

We had to *become explorers!* In this arena, talking just isn't enough. We actually had to explore each other's bodies and discover what felt good and what we didn't like. Doesn't that sound simple? Yes! Was it simple? *No!* Remember, before marriage we felt guilty if we "over" touched. Guilt is accompanied by a fear that we can't perform or won't be exciting to our mate. One discovery we made that helped us and can help any married couple is to plan times of "non-demand touching," exploring each other's body to see how good we can make the other feel. The goal is not sexual union—as a matter of fact, for this exercise sexual intercourse is forbidden! This helped us to relax, took off all the pressure of performance, and allowed us to get to know each other in a more intimate way.

We became *readers and learners.* Thirty years ago there weren't many "how-to" books, but we managed to find a few. We liked the ones that had illustrations. This helped us to be brave enough to try different positions for lovemaking. Not all were successful, but along the way we began to learn what worked for us. The Bible gives us the utmost freedom to be creative in marital lovemaking. There are no rules, no regulations, and no instructions on positions, foreplay, or frequency of sexual intercourse. The guiding principle is that it is pleasurable for both. Hebrews puts it this way: "Keep the marriage bed undefiled" (13:4).

We learned to be *others centered.* In the sexual side of marriage it's easy to become "me centered" and lose our sensitivity to our partner. We forget that the best way to really please ourselves is to please our mate. Jesus said it is more blessed to give than to receive. This is true in the sexual relationship as well as in the totality of life. We found that when we focused on pleasing the other, we were less self-conscious and even overcame some of our inhibitions. We tried to learn all we could about what turned each other on. We found that Dave tended to be visual while Claudia responded to tenderness and talk.

How Long to Adjust?

We have heard that it takes up to six years for a married couple to adjust sexually and up to twenty years to enjoy each other fully. How long have you been married? Six months? Five years? Twenty years? Let's say you have been married for five years. Do you have five years of expertise in this area or one year's expertise repeated five times? Is your sexual relationship growing? What are you doing to make your marriage a love affair? If you're not at the love affair level with your mate, we'd like to help you put romance into your love life.

It's Your Turn

Think back to your wedding night and the first years of your marriage. You may want to jot down some of your memories in the following exercise.

**REMEMBERING OUR
EARLY MARRIAGE**

The things I remember most vividly about our early marriage days are:

_____

_____

_____

_____

Did you identify with some of our memories? Or perhaps you identify more with our friends who are both highly sexual people. They can respond to each other sexually even in the middle of a serious conflict. Their sex life holds them together and requires little effort to make it run smoothly.

On the other end of the spectrum are the couple so disappointed with sex that they relegated it to the back burner and chose to work on other areas in their marriage and never made it past those initial adjustments. Maybe children arrived quickly or they just never got around to working things out.

The "S" Word in the Twenties and Thirties . . .

About the time things began to settle out for us sexually, the kids started arriving, and we started dreaming about that day way in the future when there would be fewer interruptions and much more energy. We handled our sex life and the first baby without too much stress, but when our second child arrived, things got complicated.

Psychologists tell us that the two times of greatest stress on a marriage are when you have toddlers and again when you have teens. If you have both, you have an extra challenge to keep it all together!

For us the hardest time in our sexual relationship was when we had three children ages five and under. Dave, the night owl, eagerly looked forward to lovemaking after the baby's late night feeding. Claudia, the morning lark, barely survived feeding the baby, and all she wanted after that was sleep—blessed sleep. Missing each other's expectations just made us grumpy in the morning. Actually Claudia would have been more up for sex at five in the morning, but Dave was asleep and the baby was crying. We both began to wonder if this was "natural" birth control?

Maybe you find yourself in a similar stressful situation. Your children are draining your energy, or maybe you don't have children but you're both working extremely hard in your careers. Time for loving is elusive and rare. Fortunately for us, in those stressful years we could still talk about the "S" word and both wanted to find a solution to our dilemma. Maybe some of our helpful discoveries will also help you. Yes, there was a solution, and things did get better.

To help determine how you're doing, take our SAT (Sexual Attitude Test).

TAKING THE SAT

Check the following statements that apply to you. Give yourself one point for each statement checked.

___ "I enjoy my sexual relationship with my mate."

___ "I think he or she enjoys it too."

___ "I look forward to the next time of physical intimacy."

___ "My mate tells me that he or she is satisfied with our sexual relationship."

___ "I'm satisfied with our sexual relationship."

___ "I initiate lovemaking from time to time."

___ "I plan special times for us to be alone together."

___ "We have gone off overnight alone together in the last six months."

___ "I tell my mate verbally that I desire him or her."

___ "My mate would describe me as a tender lover."

___ "I'm willing to work on areas in our sexual relationship that need improvement."

If you checked seven or more of these statements, you most likely have a reasonably good sexual relationship. If your score was lower than seven, don't be discouraged. A candid self-appraisal and an effort to modify your attitude can result in a change in your score in a very short time!

Note: On this SAT you can miss checking one of the statements and still be a "ten."

A Fulfilling Sexual Relationship Takes Work

Where do we get the idea that we enter marriage with built-in "know how"? We learn to respond sexually, as we learn in anything else, by working at it. We wouldn't assume built-in knowledge in childrearing, our professions, or hanging wallpaper! No, achieving success in any endeavor requires work, and sex is no exception.

A Fulfilling Sexual Relationship Takes Understanding

We don't marry into an instant understanding of each other. Before we were married, we felt we knew and understood just about everything about each other. But later we discovered there were new discoveries and areas we had to work at in understanding each other. Our friends Helen and Pete love each other and want to have a good sexual relationship, but they need help in understanding how they are different. Check out this scenario:

Helen decided to make this night special. Lately their sexual relationship had been sort of bland, and she decided to spice it up. "First," she thought, "I'll pick up Pete's favorite Chinese food, pull out the china and silver, and even use linen napkins and light the candles." She followed her good intentions with action and even splurged on a manicure. When Pete walked in the door, soft music played in the background, and Helen was ready!

What about Pete? The main thing on his agenda was getting home to see the NBA final on television. At lunch Pete and his management team had talked about the basketball final. He knew his team had a great chance to win it. His agenda was to get home, turn on the TV, pull up a TV tray, and watch his favorite team take the championship!

Helen and Pete had different expectations for the evening—neither good nor bad but definitely conflicting.

When Pete arrived home, Helen was ready for a passionate kiss and bear hug. Instead she got a quick peck as Pete headed straight for the TV. Talk about expectations! They were in conflict, but neither understood the other's hopes. The evening went downhill from there. Pete was so into the ballgame that he was missing Helen's act. A drama was being played and he didn't even know he was the villain!

Later as they were preparing to go to bed, Helen began to undress. Pete is a visual type of guy, and just seeing his wife undress caused his blood to flow. As he began to show a little loving initiative, Helen ran out of the bedroom in tears!

What was Pete's crime? He and Helen failed to understand their expectations and the different way they responded to each other. Pete was stimulated by sight. If Helen had been a "total woman" and met him at the door in a raincoat (only), he might not have made it to the NBA final on TV. On the other hand, if Pete had given Helen the tenderness and chatter she desired, her response could have been different too.

What about you? What puts you in a loving mood? What about your mate? You may want to stop and talk about it right now.

LOVING MOOD INSTIGATORS

The things that tend to put me in a loving mood are:

1. _____
2. _____
3. _____

The things that I think put my mate in a loving mood are:

1. _____
2. _____
3. _____

A Fulfilling Sexual Relationship Takes Time

Too often what happens is that other things take precedence over the sexual relationship. You want to work on it but don't set aside time to spend alone together. Remember, it takes time to communicate, to work through conflict, and to build a creative love life. Ten minutes after the ball game on TV just won't do. Let us encourage you to commit yourselves to taking the time and making the effort to make sex a growing, exciting part of your marriage. It can happen!

We started by carving out a regular time each week when we could be alone without the children. Having an office in our home proved advantageous. One year we instigated our "Monday Mornings." All three children were in kindergarten or Mom's Day Out and we had full run of the house. We discovered that there is nothing sacred about making love at night. Monday mornings were great! Your schedule may not be as flexible as ours, but you need to find the time that works for you and plan it! For example, maybe you can hire a baby-sitter to take your kids out for a couple of hours Saturday mornings.

We also started the tradition of going off alone together. We began to realize we needed extended times alone together—more than just a morning. So we began to look for opportunities to plan just-for-two getaways. We couldn't afford to hire a sitter to come and stay with our children for an extended time, and our parents lived too far away. But we did have friends—very good friends—who offered to keep our three Indians. We reciprocated by keeping their two girls, and we're sure we got the better deal!

Years later two of our early getaways stand out in our memories, but for very different reasons. The first was a weekend we went to a cabin in Alabama. This was our first weekend to get away alone, and it was "love city" from the time we got there to the time we left! Dave remembers the

Alabama weekend as very fulfilling. Claudia remembers being oh so exhausted.

The second getaway we especially remember is the week we spent at the beach in Florida. Claudia fondly remembers the slow pace of life, the long walks on the beach, romantic interludes, candlelit dinners for two, and shopping together and buying a new dress. Dave remembers it as a great week too, but years later confided he was a little disappointed that we didn't make love every day we were there.

If we could live those years over again, we would talk more about our expectations and what is realistic for us. The key is to find balance and to come up with your own unique plan. While you're parenting toddlers, a fulfilling sexual relationship is not going to happen spontaneously!

You may want to take a few minutes right now and talk about your unique situation and what you can do to make your marriage more of a love affair. Take a tip from the Arps and do talk about our expectations. When you plan a getaway for two, you may want to talk about which of our getaways you identify with more—the cabin in Alabama or the beach in Florida? Where in your weekly schedule can you carve out some just-for-two loving time?

OUR LOVE AFFAIR

Ways we can make our marriage more of a love affair:

1. _____

2. _____

3. _____

4. _____

Sex in the Late Thirties and Forties

Let's jump ahead a few years, past the late-night feedings. The "S" word is still around. Now our own teenage fantasies and sexual dreams become nightmares and fears for our own teenagers. We pray daily they will have the self-restraint that was so difficult to find in our own dating and premarriage years.

That elusive and subtle fear may enter our bedroom. We may become more guarded around our adolescents. After all, we don't want them to get any ideas from us about how enjoyable sex is. Because we are so fearful that our children will become sexually involved, we may, without realizing it, lower the priority of the "S" word.

Please don't misunderstand us. We don't advocate parading our sex life (or lack of it) in front of our kids. But we can pass on positive attitudes about sex to the products of our family planning. Whenever the "S" word came up in family conversations, we openly told our sons that sex in marriage is one of God's greatest gifts. It's okay to let your kids know that you know skin on skin feels good. At the same time we stressed that they were not adults. The "S" word is reserved for marriage and for adults! We were encouraged when one of our sons filled out a high school form and put "not before marriage" in the blank that said sex.

We do know that attitudes are caught, not taught. It's not so much what you say as what you model. Do you openly give and receive physical affection? In *How to Really Love Your Child,* Dr. Ross Campbell talks about the importance of filling your child's emotional tank with hugs and kisses.

This is just as important for mates—especially when you have teens! One of Dave's best childhood memories is seeing his parents out on the balcony kissing and hugging each other. In the days of epidemic divorce, kids feel secure when they are assured—not just by words—that Mom and Dad really do love each other.

The adolescent years can add stress to any marriage. So we found some ways to combat that stress in our sexual relationship.

We needed to protect our own attitude toward sex. Even though sexual activity was not appropriate for our adolescents, we affirmed it was still right and appropriate and important to our marriage relationship.

We made a commitment not to let our teenagers crowd out our "alone time." Some of the ways we found that time were:

1. Use times when your adolescents are at school activities. (You don't have to be at every ball game they sub in!)
2. Look for alone time—like when your teens sleep in on Saturday morning.
3. Soundproof your own bedroom. A stereo system or radio provides a noise buffer and adds to your privacy.

Don't let your teen's problems totally overwhelm you. Sometimes we can get too caught up in our children's situations. After all, this is a temporary stage. They do grow up and they do leave home. You want to nurture and enjoy your sexual relationship with your mate all of your married life, so don't let the stresses of life with adolescents short circuit it!

Develop a sense of humor. Sometimes in family life you have to either laugh or cry. When faced with that choice, we tried to laugh. Laughter dispels tension and actually helps us relax. During those years we tried not to take ourselves too seriously and to realize that much we were experiencing was temporary.

Do the unexpected! During these intense years, you can add the element of surprise by doing the unexpected. We've been known to do some zany things ourselves. Claudia will never forget the day Dave came in with three red roses and said, "Pack your bag. We're leaving in thirty minutes!" Remember, Dave is the romantic!

Off we went to a wonderful little hotel in the Vienna woods about thirty minutes from where we lived. Claudia wondered why they looked at her so curiously when we checked in. Dave had previously chosen the hotel and told them he had a very special lady friend he wanted to bring for a getaway. To this day, Claudia is convinced that the staff didn't think we were married. Dave's reaction? "If you're going to have a romantic affair, have it with your mate!" And that's just what we did.

Now think about your marriage. What are you doing to build a creative love life? Waiting for the children to grow up and leave home is not an appropriate answer! Or if your answer is, "It's just not that important to us," we'd like to challenge your thinking. Take it from us, this part of marriage can grow and become more enjoyable and fulfilling every year!

Love Life in the Fifties and Sixties

One friend said, "By the time you've gotten to the empty nest, you have forgotten how to spell the "S" word. We are now in the empty nest. For years we have looked forward to the extra freedom and flexibility we would have in our sexual life when our last son left home. It does have its benefits!

We hadn't forgotten the "S" word, but we had developed the habit of work, work, and more work. Some of the time vacated by our son was swallowed by more book deadlines, marriage workshops, and parenting groups. The whole house was now available to us. We could venture out, but our lifestyle was too busy to take advantage of our new freedom. We simply tried to do more!

Again we needed to work to add some creativity to our love life. We tried to slow down and even reclaim our den with the fireplace. Old habits die hard. If you are a driven workaholic, your love life may suffer. Here are some ideas we have found helpful.

Try new things. Move your lovemaking to new settings. Try out all the rooms in your house and see what appeals to you. For instance:

- Maybe one of your kids who flew the nest left a waterbed behind.
- Consider that swing you just added to your secluded screened porch.
- Why not initiate the new carpet?
- Love under bubbles in a candlelit bubble bath?
- A whole evening of nondemand touching.
- A game in which the loser must strip—one game you can both win!

All these suggestions are not from the Arps. We heard some of them at a follow-up group of one of our Marriage Alive Workshops. The workshop had taken place eight months before and this particular group had gotten together each month to share and encourage one another to stay on the marriage track. That they had been successful was evidenced by this particular evening.

Each couple had been asked to bring one thing that represented their marriage. One couple brought a beautiful green potted plant to suggest a healthy and growing marriage. Another couple brought a devotional book and shared how they were now having devotions and praying together. This, they said, had deepened their commitment to God and to each other.

Amazingly, over half of the group shared something about adding creativity to their love life. From hotel receipts to whipped cream—this group was creative. But one couple took the prize. They brought a tuxedo apron, a chef's hat, and a bottle of lotion. They were in the empty nest and both worked outside the home. On this evening the husband had volunteered for kitchen duty and begun to prepare dinner. The wife, exhausted, stretched out on the newly carpeted living room floor and fell asleep. Imagine her surprise when her husband woke her up wearing only the tuxedo apron and chef's hat, with lotion in hand all ready to give her a body massage! Creativity was alive and well at their home.

Another couple took a picnic basket full of goodies to eat and checked in at a local hotel. The money they spent on the hotel was a great investment in their marriage team.

Another thing we have discovered about this stage of life is the importance of doing what we can do to stay healthy and physically fit. We didn't come up with this on our own. Several years ago, Claudia hurt her back. For several weeks she was out of commission. It wasn't fun, but one benefit of this "down" time was our new determination to improve our physical condition. We used to play lots of tennis, but somehow had just let it slip. So we started walking together and even doing some weight training together. Now we definitely have more energy for the "fun" things in life!

A friend of ours decided to take an empty nest inventory of her clothes, especially her underwear. Out went the dowdy duds and lace was back in.

You may not like all of our suggestions, and that's fine.

But we hope you like some of them. If you seriously want to deepen your sexual relationship, make this area a priority. Begin by checking your schedule. Make sure you guard your "together alone" time. You'll never add creativity to your love life unless you have some uninterrupted blocks of time alone.

Also let us encourage you to be sensitive to one another. Have you ever been on a diet? What do you think about all the time? Food! When we aren't sensitive to our partner's sexual needs, we are putting him or her on a diet—and guess what he or she thinks about all the time. That's right—sex!

A friend of ours asked her doctor what he felt was the major sexual problem in marriage. He said half of his patients complained that their mates never bothered them about sex, while the other half complained that their mates bothered them too much about sex. He said that if only he could reshuffle the couples, everyone would be happy!

Perhaps you don't agree with each other about the frequency of sexual intercourse. Here is one place to use those communication skills you learned in Chapter 4. Discuss this area openly, but remember that the key is to be sensitive to the needs of the other person.

"LET ME TELL YOU HOW I FEEL"

Using the feelings formula in Style Four Communication, express your feelings. You may want to write out how you feel. (For example, "I feel that we need to make love more often. What do you think about making that a goal for the next month and planning some special times together?")

I feel _____

_____

_____

Be willing to take the initiative. Consider making the arrangements for a weekend away, or plan a couple of hours each week when you can be completely alone. Don't overlook the possibility of using a friend's empty apartment for a date.

After you have chosen to make this a priority area and have carved out the time, you may want to try some of these ideas:

1. Call your mate to express your desire for him or her.
2. Write your mate a love letter.
3. Give your mate an all-over body massage with scented lotion.
4. Spend at least one hour talking and loving each other.
5. Have your mate verbalize what pleases him or her.
6. Give your mate an unexpected little gift for no reason at all.
7. Buy a new "mood music" tape or CD.
8. Tell your mate ten reasons you love him or her.
9. Take an inventory of your bedroom and make any needed changes to add to the romantic atmosphere like adding candles, music, a light dimmer switch, a lock on the door. Remove all

those books and paper work—find them another
home, and forget about your "to-do" list when
you are "behind closed doors."
10. Make arrangements now to go away overnight.

We have even been known to use our adult offspring's
apartment! One summer when Jarrett and Laurie were going to be away for several weeks, they offered us their apartment in Williamsburg, Virginia, for a getaway. We took them
up on it. Imagine our surprise when we walked in and saw
the table romantically set for two with candles and china.

We hope you will take our advice and continue to work
on enriching your love life.

Sex in the Seventies and Eighties?

Recently we visited an elderly couple, both in their
eighties, both hard of hearing. It was hard to have a conversation with them over the television. They didn't want to
miss their soaps, and on this day the soaps were hot and
steamy! From the hot tub, to the waterbed, to the beach, the
"S" word was acted out with passion and fury. We began to
realize that sex is still a focal point even in the senior years!
But most elderly are experiencing it vicariously.

We plan to be the exception, and if we are we'll write a
book about it! In the meantime, we're going to keep working
on our sexual relationship. To be honest, we are not to the
soap opera stage. With all the "soap" passion and excitement, we wonder why those characters don't have heart attacks right and left! If sex is all that great all the time, the
Arps are missing out, and probably you are too!

We conclude by confessing to you that our lovemaking
is usually fine, sometimes fantastic, but always enjoyable.
As the years go by, it keeps getting better, and we look for-

ward to enjoying each other in our sixties, seventies, and eighties. If we have heart attacks, we can only say, "What a way to go!"

What about you? It's your choice. Your sexual relationship can be as fulfilling and exciting as you want to make it. You will find it takes time and work. But it's worth it; it can become better, more intimate, and more wonderful as the years go on!

TRACKING TOGETHER

Learning to Say the "S" Word

Purpose:

To become more creative on our love life

To talk more openly in this area

Preparation:

Review Chapter 7, "Learning to Say the 'S' Word"

Fill out exercises and be ready to discuss

Our Tracking Time is:

Date and Time _____

Location _____

What needs to be done to make it happen:

1. _____

2. _____

3. _____

Tracking-together Time:

Together discuss the following exercises:

1. My "Sex Education" (p. 109)
2. Remembering Our Early Marriage (p. 116)
3. Taking the SAT (p. 117)
4. Loving Mood Instigators (p. 120)
5. Our Love Affair (p. 122)
6. "Let Me Tell You How I Feel" (p. 128)

CHAPTER EIGHT

Working with Your Working Mate

I f we only had more hours in our days, we could balance the two-job tightrope!" commented Ed and Katie Brown. This particular Marriage Alive Workshop, filled with two-career couples, was also filled with frustrations evidenced by Ed and Katie's comment.

Telling them that they had time—in fact, all the time there is—didn't solve their dilemma. However, that particular workshop session did help them come up with a workable plan. If you are among the 58 percent of marrieds who are trying to balance jobs outside the home, we hope this chapter will help you get a better handle on your two-job team and come up with a plan that works for you.[1]

You may think this chapter doesn't relate to you because you're not working outside the home. But if your five preschoolers—give or take a few kids—make an outside job look like a vacation don't skip this chapter! You, too, can benefit from looking closer at how you can work with your working mate.

Stop, and think of all the things we blame on time. How many times have you said:

"If I just had more time . . ."
"I'll have time for that when . . .
   . . . the children grow up
   . . . the summer comes
   . . . the summer is over
   . . . I meet this deadline or finish this project (for us, when we finish this book)."

May we suggest time is not the real culprit? Time really is no respecter of persons. It's impartial. We don't have more time each day than you do. Every single person on this earth has twenty-four hours every day—no more or no less! The real issues are how we manage our time and how we work together to balance our two-job team? To help you answer this question, it's time for a "time out" to take inventory!

The first step in working with your working mate is to look at where you are and assess your real situation. To help you do just that, complete the following exercise.

ASSESSING OUR RESPONSIBILITIES

Responsibilities Outside of the Home

1. _____   1. _____

2. _____   2. _____

3. _____   3. _____

4. _____   4. _____

Responsibilities Inside the Home

1. _____   1. _____

2. _____   2. _____

3. _____   3. _____

4. _____   4. _____

If you arranged all your various responsibilities on a seesaw, putting yours on one end and your mate's on the other, how would your seesaw balance? For instance, if one mate is working outside the home only part-time each week and the other is working a sixty-hour week, the one who is home part-time would need to balance the seesaw by carrying more of the load at home. But for now, let's assume you both have equal commitments outside the home. The important question is, "How are you pulling together as a team at home?"

In spite of many unrealistic stereotypes today—especially of the "macho males" who don't get their hands wet—the younger generation has one up on our age group. We are delighted to see our two married couples pulling together as teams as they wrestle with grad school, jobs, and busy schedules.

On the other hand, consider Ed and Katie. They are our vintage and grew up with stereotypes of men doing this and women doing that. The traditional roles worked well for them when their three kids were little and Katie chose to stay home and be a full-time mom. But halfway through the parenting years, their circumstances changed. Ed's company took an economic slide, and their finances suffered. Although she preferred to stay at home, Katie reluctantly took a teaching job to help meet expenses and begin saving for future educational needs.

This mid-course adjustment really didn't change Ed's routine very much at all. He still was working as hard as ever at his job and came home just as tired. Katie was a different story. Now five days a week she came home tired, had lesson plans to prepare for the next day, and also had all the jobs at home staring at her—the least of which was what were they going to have each night for dinner. Ed was understanding and didn't say much about the frozen dinners, but not having clean socks was a little too much for him. Tension began to build, and by the time Ed and Katie came to our marriage workshop, they needed help!

A light seemed to go on when Ed and Katie did the above exercise and looked at their home seesaw. It looked something like this:

Responsibilities at Home

Katie	Ed
1. Prepare meals	1. Take care of the yard
2. Grocery shop	2. Keep cars maintained
3. Do laundry for family	3. Keep family financial
4. Keep the house clean	records
5. Arrange for sitters	
6. Help children with homework	

It was evident that Ed and Katie needed to make some adjustments. Ed's home responsibilities were important and took time, but he could accomplish them on the weekends. Katie's areas of responsibility were not as flexible and daily demanded more than she could give after a day of teaching school. They needed help in balancing home responsibilities.

Maybe you're in the same dilemma. If so, let us walk you through the exercise that helped Ed and Katie.

BALANCING HOME RESPONSIBILITIES

The first step is to list all household jobs and responsibilities (like meal preparation, cleaning the house, laundry, helping children with homework, caring for the yard).

Major responsibilities in our home are:

1. _____

2. _____

3. _____

4. _____

5. _____

6. _____

7. _____

8. _____

Look at the above list together and decide:

What I like to do best:

1. _____

2. _____

3. _____

4. _____

What I like to do least:

1. _____

2. _____

3. _____

4. _____

When we Arps did this exercise, we listed all the various jobs and chores and then went through the list together from the grid of who can do the job better. Claudia immediately conceded that Dave was the best bathroom cleaner in ten states! The brutal reality is that no one will choose or want to do some jobs! Compromise is an important part of the process, and don't forget creativity. Who *is* going to clean the bathroom? When no one immediately volunteers, it's time to brainstorm. List possibilities (Humor helps the process!).

Possible solution to dirty bathrooms:

1. Husband cleans bathroom.
2. Wife cleans bathroom.
3. Husband and wife rotate cleaning the bathroom.
4. Teach the children to clean bathroom.
5. Hire it done.
6. Don't use bathroom.

7. Make a chart and let each family member have a cleaning day.
8. Each person cleans the bathroom (tub, sink, etc.) after using it.

Remember, you are trying to attack the extra pressures of having a two-job team, instead of attacking each other. You are also looking for understanding. We can all handle stress better if just one other person understands how we feel. You can be that other person for your mate.

Once Ed and Katie did the exercise, Ed became more aware of the stress Katie was experiencing and the need for his increased involvement in the home. The solution to his "no clean socks dilemma" might be to wash them himself! But the mechanics of who does what are not as important as the philosophy of a team attacking the problem together.

Katie and Ed's children were school age and were recruited for jobs around the house. They were even assigned responsibility for the bathroom! Katie was tired of teaching when she arrived home in the afternoons and loved being creative in the kitchen. She invested in some new cookbooks for easy one-dish meals. She also pulled out the crockpot and with a little planning often had dinner on the way before she left for school in the morning. Ed began to monitor homework and help with special school assignments.

For the heavy jobs around the house, Katie and Ed had a cleaning service come in once a month. They also found a high school boy who loved yard work and did the routine mowing and mulching. Ed and Katie's seesaw may still go up and down, but on any given day it's much more balanced.

Till Debt Do Us Part

One point of contention in a two-career home is finances. One wife we know went to work, as Katie did, to help with financial difficulty. But this wife's working added to their financial tension. Listen to her story:

"When I went back to work, I thought I'd have some income of my own. But what actually happened is that it all went into the same pot. My husband won't tell me where we are financially, and it's driving me crazy. I'd be better off if I just had my own bank account and helped with our general expenses."

This couple needed to take some time and figure out how to work out their finances together. They needed to come up with a financial plan they both could agree to and to decide if separate accounting would help or hurt.

At different times in our marriage, we've handled the bank account issue in different ways. When we were first married, it was all we could do to keep up with one bank account. Then as our life became more complicated, we had separate accounts we were each responsible for. Dave's account covered things like house payments or rent, utilities and other monthly bills, savings, and insurance premiums. From Claudia's account, she paid for groceries, household items, and clothing. Together we decided what our basic budget should be and how much we wanted to save and to give to our church and to others. Later we added another account that we call our "special" account. Money in our special account is for giving to others and for special needs.

For us the real concern is not how many bank accounts we have (separate or joint) or even how much money we have, but that we have a workable financial plan that we both agree to. If you function best with separate accounts and it works for you, great!

It helps greatly to have defined financial goals. These should be goals that you mutually agree on. We remember when we bought our first house—today it would be hard to buy a car for the amount we paid for our first home—but for us, it was a huge goal to come up with a down payment. Claudia was a substitute teacher in a local high school, and we were able to save her paychecks toward our house down payment.

In setting financial goals and working hard together to achieve them, let us add one caution: It is possible to end up with all the things we would like to have, but no time to enjoy them. Working with our working mate can become slavery to maintaining all our possessions. We can have it all and actually have nothing.

Dr. M. Scott Peck, author of *The Road Less Traveled,* points out that a sign of maturity is the ability to delay gratification. Yet we live in an instant world—instant oatmeal, instant coffee, and instant credit. Continually we hear that we can have it all and have it right now. If you are bored and have the right credit card, you can whisk your mate off to a romantic island—no need to get baby-sitters (if you have children) or even pack. We are told to "Just do it!" Many problems in marriage could be lessened if we just learned to delay gratification!

We make no claims of being financial advisors. To be honest, we don't have it all together in this area, but we are working on it, so we can share with you some things that are helping us. One of the best and most practical books on finances is Ron Blue's *Managing Your Money.®* We highly recommend using this book as a basic guide. If you use a computer, another helpful tool is the program *Manage Your Money.*[2]

Other things we have tried that have helped us are:

1. From time to time keep a detailed record of each penny you spend. We have done this for up to five or six months. Then it is easy to evaluate where

your money is going and to modify spending and saving patterns, which is not so easy, but possible.

2. Limit credit card spending to what you can pay off each month. If things are really tight, we try not to use credit cards. Somehow, it's just easier to justify buying with a credit card. We sometimes say "Well, I'll probably bring it back and it'll be easier to return if I charge it." One thing is sure—it will be easier to buy—but a month later the bill arrives.

3. Don't overlook the joy of giving. Several couples we know also have a special account at the bank. Each month they place a certain amount of money in that account, and from it they support their church and several missionaries and ministries.

4. Get in the habit of saving. We used to say we just couldn't afford to save. The truth is we can't afford not to save. How much we save is not as critical as developing the habit of saving. Consider choosing long-term goals—such as retirement and your children's education. Also choose short-term goals. If you have older children, you may want together to choose a family goal to work towards. For instance you might have a family garage sale to help finance a special family vacation.

Choose Your Own Lifestyle Carefully

Only you can decide this highly personal issue for your marriage team. But the two of you should make the decision together. To help you think through different issues, you may want to talk through what your necessities are. This will be different for each couple. A starting place in evaluating this question is to think back to when you first got married and compare your living standards then and now.

BALANCING OUR WANTS AND NEEDS

What we had when we   What we have today:
first got married:

_____   _____

_____   _____

_____   _____

_____   _____

What is most important to us? Consider the following areas (by no means a comprehensive list). Give each a rating, like, 3 = very important; 2 = nice to have but not so important; or 1 = can live without it.

____ House
____ Car
____ Household appliances (You may want to list and evaluate each individually.)
____ Television
____ VCR
____ Stereo equipment
____ Household help
____ Vacations
____ Eating out
____ Entertainment, (movies, sports, etc.)

Other things may also be necessities, but are less tangible.

___ Time with each other
___ Time with children
___ Time with friends
___ Church
___ Sports
___ Community service

Life Involves Choices

One young family we know was continually struggling to meet house payments and other obligations. Before the children appeared, both worked, and they really had not felt a lot of financial stress. The wife wanted to stay home with their two young daughters, but economically it seemed impossible. After working through an exercise like the one above, they listed their priorities. Home ownership was great, but higher on their list was for one of them to be at home to love and nurture their young children.

What they did was brave. They sold their house and moved back into an apartment so Pat could stay home with their children. Tough choices await each of us. But the good news is that we do have choices. There is lots of room for creativity, and in today's world we need every bit of it!

What Will You Choose?

Some of us have more choices than others, but we all have to make choices. Katie went back to work to help provide for their family in a needy time. Another chose to pursue a career. Pat chose to stay home to nurture their preschoolers. No one can tell you what is right or wrong for you.

Whatever your situation, please, oh please, look for

ways to make time for each other. If you both work outside the home, do it from a united front. You'll need all the communication and negotiating skills you can muster. You will continually need to evaluate your expectations and redefine your goals. Don't be like the couple who were going to build their relationship, but there just wasn't time. Raising five kids kept them busy, but in the empty nest, they still rarely saw each other. They were both in jobs that required traveling and weren't really aware of how disjointed their lives had become. One day they met accidentally in the Los Angeles Airport. Neither even knew the other was supposed to be in California! Just then the obvious hit them: We don't even know each other; we have homes, cars, boats, but we don't have an alive marriage. From that important turning point, they looked at their lives and decided it was time to make some changes; they are now working through their necessity list and eliminating some other things. It will take a lot of work and commitment, but they are on the right track!

We often hear, "We're doing it all for our kids—to give them advantages in life." A noted child psychologist on a TV morning program said one key to successful parenting is to spend half as much money on your kids and twice as much time! Let us expand and refocus this comment: The key to a growing, alive marriage is to spend half as much money on things and twice as much time with your mate! It's up to you to work together to chart your course.

TRACKING TOGETHER

Working with Your Working Mate

Purpose:
> To look at how we share responsibilities
> To balance responsibilities and pull together as a team
> To look at our finances and balance wants and needs

Preparation:
> Review Chapter 8, "Working with Your Working Mate"
> Fill out exercises and be ready to discuss

Our Tracking Time is:
> Date and Time _____
>
> Location _____

What needs to be done to make it happen:
> 1. _____
> 2. _____
> 3. _____

Tracking-together Time:
> Together discuss the following exercises:
> 1. Assessing Our Responsibilities (p. 134)
> 2. Balancing Home Responsibilities (p. 137)
> 3. Balancing Our Wants and Needs (p. 143)

CHAPTER NINE

Getting Back On When You Jump Track

We knew that this Marriage Alive conference was going to be tough when one participant said at the beginning of the session on conflict, "We have no conflict in our marriage because I'm always right!" Another added, "All my wife has to do is tell me her problem, and I'll solve it!" The nonverbal message from his mate was "Just try and solve my problems!"

No one gets married to add conflict to life. Quite the contrary. The premarital stars usually block thoughts of future conflict. That's one reason it's difficult to teach engaged couples how to resolve conflict. They know they are the exception! Once married, however, you've got to learn skills to survive or you'll drown.

To avoid all unpleasant conversations and issues may keep the peace, but it also keeps and extends the distance in a relationship. Yet often, when we try to reach a resolution, we become angry and frustrated and find ourselves back in Style Two Communication—attacking!

Marriage specialist Dr. David Mace says in *Love and Anger in Marriage* that the biggest problem in marriage is not lack of communication but the inability to handle and process anger. Look at the diagram below.[1]

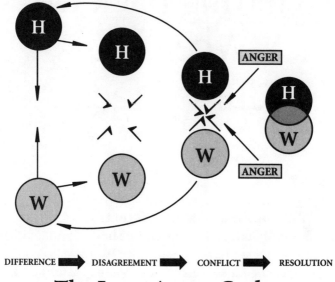

DIFFERENCE ➡ DISAGREEMENT ➡ CONFLICT ➡ RESOLUTION

The Love-Anger Cycle

H represents the husband, and W represents the wife. When couples are dating they are on the left side of the chart. There is a lot of space in their relationship. They are not together continually, but they want to be! After marriage, with less space, there are more opportunities for disagreements and for sparks to fly. The goal is to resolve the conflict causing the anger and to break through to the right side of the diagram to intimacy. But often the conflict is not resolved, and each pulls back to the left side, giving the other spouse more space. As couples repeat this love-anger cycle, walls begin to grow. The list of things "we just don't talk about" grows as well, and intimacy in marriage is just a pipe dream.

Where are you on this chart? Perhaps you find yourself caught in the love-anger cycle and would like to get out of it. The good news is that you can break out of this cycle and move toward intimacy if you are willing to take the risk and work at resolving the conflict causing the anger. To begin, look at how you presently handle conflict.

How Do You Handle Conflict?

We hate to admit it, but too often we handle conflict like some of our animal friends. Do you see yourself in these inappropriate methods!

The Turtle—The Withdrawer

Dave is the turtle in our family. When faced with a conflict situation, Dave's normal reaction is to withdraw. He just pulls his head inside his hard shell for the duration. Claudia, who occasionally likes a heated verbal interchange, can beat on his shell, but to no avail.

Are you a turtle? Do you usually withdraw from conflict? You may withdraw physically, like getting up and walking out of the room, or you may withdraw emotionally, by turning the other person off. Maybe you feel hopeless and that you can't win anyway, so why discuss it? Let us give you a word of caution: Withdrawing turns off the relationship as well as a possible solution and moves you very quickly to the left side of the love-anger cycle!

The Skunk—The Attacker

Do you identify with the skunk? The skunk is a master of sarcasm and is usually very quick verbally. He or she would rather make the other person look bad than deal with any personal shortcomings.

Claudia is much more like a skunk. Her favorite approach is to attack Dave and to make him stink first! She would rather focus on what he did or didn't do and avoid any responsibility on her part!

Over the years of leading Marriage Alive Workshops, we've met a lot of turtles who are married to skunks. We've even observed a new breed—the skirtle. The skirtle is a combination of the skunk and the turtle. How does the skirtle handle conflict? By attacking the other person and then retreating into his or her shell!

The Chameleon—The Yielder

The chameleon turns colors to blend into the environment, thus avoiding conflict. He agrees with whatever opinions are being expressed. When he is with a quiet group, he is quiet too. When he is with a loud group, he becomes loud. His desire to fit in and be accepted prevents him from expressing his real opinion, so when he meets conflict, he'll go along with the crowd.

Often this is the mate who leaves a marriage after thirty years of "giving in." No one can understand what triggered his or her departure because he or she always adapted so convincingly.

The Owl—The Intellectualizer

The owl, like the turtle, tries to avoid conflict. His methods are just different. He is the intellectualizer; his motto is "Avoid feelings at all cost!" The owl will gladly discuss an issue on an intellectual basis, but he has no feelings from his cranium down. He deals with facts, facts, and facts!

The Gorilla—The Winner

The gorilla has to win at all costs. His two favorite weapons are manipulation and intimidation. Underneath his tough skin is a person who may be very insecure and wants to look good no matter what the cost. He keeps files of old grudges, hurts, and wrongs to be pulled out and used at the appropriate times. He loves to tell you what is wrong with everything and why he is right!

We'll never forget the workshop when one participant turned out to be the classic gorilla. We barely made it through each session because of Bill's constant interruption to correct us and tell us what we were doing wrong—or how we could do it better "his way." He continually attacked and put down his wife. The solution came from among the participants. During a break, several of them slipped away and came back with a huge bunch of bananas for Bill, the gorilla. He finally got the message! Did he make a drastic change for the better? Not really, but he is working on modifying his style and the following exercises helped him to do it.

What's Your Style?

Do you identify with any of our animal friends? You may identify with more than one of them. We often react to conflict in different ways at different times. The following exercise will help you look at how you presently handle conflict. Note: this exercise is diagnostic and is intended to help you see more clearly how you presently handle conflict. Later in this chapter, we will walk together through the practical steps of how to resolve an honest conflict.

HOW DO YOU HANDLE ANGER?

Answer the following three questions.

1. How do I feel when I get angry (for example, frustrated, misunderstood, let down, or alone)?

   When I get angry I feel _____

   _____

   _____

2. What do I do when I become angry? We still remember the time during the first year of our marriage when Claudia threw the Salvo soap at Dave. (Salvo was soap in bullet form. It's no longer available—we guess it was just too dangerous!)

   When I become angry, I am (a turtle who withdraws, a skunk who attacks, a chameleon who yields, an owl who intellectualizes, or a gorilla who must always win)

   _____

   _____

   _____

3. What would be a more appropriate response (not, as one workshop participant said, "I'd like to kill him!")? Consider the following list and check appropriate statements.

   ___ I wish I could put the "hot potato" down and let it cool.

   ___ I wish I could identify Stage Two Communication— attacking—and get out of it.

   ___ I wish I could stop the escalation of my anger.

   ___ I wish we could resolve the conflict together and move on into intimacy.

The good news is that there is hope. You can do all of the above! First we need to define areas of conflict. What issues keep coming up in our relationship? Sometimes we argue over such insignificant things. Little daily things can irritate. Don't forget the little flies in the soup:

- You like the house as warm as the tropics, and your mate would make a good Eskimo!
- You are Mr. Pro and are married to Mrs. Con (or vice versa).
- You like the toilet paper to unroll from the top, but your mate likes it to unroll from the bottom.
- Your middle name is Punctuality—your mate's is Late Arriver.
- You like that homey, lived-in look—your mate arranges the magazines on the table at a forty-five-degree angle.
- You are a precision toothpaste roller—your mate, a creative squeezer.

AREAS THAT TRIGGER CONFLICT

If little things don't make sparks fly at your house consider the following. Check areas that apply to you.

____ Money
____ Children
____ Sex
____ In-laws
____ Priorities and time management

Take a couple of minutes and list areas that trigger conflict in your relationship.

1. _____

2. _____

3. _____

4. _____

Now let's walk through the four steps you can take to resolve conflict.

Steps for Resolving Conflict

Step One: Define the Problem

It seemed like an average run-of-the-mill workshop until we got to the session on resolving honest conflict—then war erupted! We had just completed giving the participants the four-step process for resolving an issue. To bring it home, we chose what we thought was a fun simple situation to illustrate how the steps worked. We started by defining the problem: "I don't like towels left on the bathroom floor."

If looks could kill, we were already in trouble. We also observed elbow nudging and whispered comments. We chose to ignore these hints that all was not well and proceeded to step two.

Step Two: Identify Which One of You Needs a Solution and the Other's Contribution to the Problem

We arbitrarily said: "The wife has the need. The husband leaves wet towels on the floor." The "looks" told us we were about 50 percent right. We figured, when all is silent, just move on to the next point. We were digging our grave and didn't even know it!

Step Three: List Alternate Solutions

A few humorists in the group helped us compile our list:

Leave towel on floor
Wife picks up towel
Husband picks up towel
Use disposable towels and throw away
Don't use towels and drip dry
Don't bathe
Fold towel and put on rack.

As we waited patiently for group consensus that the last alternative—fold towel and put on rack—was best, war erupted. Rather than focus on the problem, the partners polarized, picked sides, and shot off verbal bullets. In this group, towels on the bathroom floor was a major emotional issue. It took us some time to get control of the group and call a truce. What went wrong? They forgot one simple principle—to attack the problem and not each other!

Step Four: Select a Plan of Action

As we attempted to resolve the war of the towels, we emphasized the need to be on the same team. Then we pointed out that when you are on the same team, there are three basic ways to reach a resolution and choose a plan of action. We call them the three C's: Compromise, Capitulation and Coexistence. Let's examine each.

The Three C's[2]

Compromise simply means we each give a little to find a solution that we both can live with. For the war of the towels, compromise might mean each person picks up his or her own towel and puts the towel back on the rack or in the hamper.

Capitulation reminds us of the army general forcing the opposing army to surrender. This is not what we mean, but there are times that issues are just more important to one person than to the other and the simplest way to resolve the conflict is for the one who doesn't have as much at stake to go along with the other. For example, recently we redid the walls in our kitchen. Claudia picked out the paint sample she liked and was convinced it was the appropriate shade of blue. Dave was just as convinced that it was purple instead of blue and couldn't imagine how it would possibly go with our decor. Since Claudia had the stronger feelings about the color of the walls and the proven expertise in this area, Dave capitulated and was not that surprised when it ended up looking great—and blue!

Coexistence, the third practical way to come to a solution, teaches us that we don't have to agree on everything. In some areas it's best simply to be different. For instance, take food preferences. Dave likes beets while Claudia thinks they stink! So imagine Dave's surprise when one summer Claudia took him on a tour of her vegetable garden and showed him the beets, which were growing just for him. Later, she confessed that she thought she was planting radishes.

Maybe you have differing political views or like different styles of music. Remember our goal is not to be alike; some differences add spice to our marriage team. At different times and in different situations, we use all three C's. The problem arises when one mate continually gives in to the other or when you choose to coexist on everything or you use compromise as a means of "horse-trading" and manipulating the other.

How can we put this all together and use these principles in a situation more vital than the war of the towels? Let's look at a dilemma we faced recently.

The Un-fun Discussion of Fund-raising

It had been a long but productive day. We spent most of the time working on our chapter on communication. Again we were impressed with how helpful it is to express our feelings and avoid attacking the other. Then it happened. Isn't there a Bible verse somewhere about just when you think you have it all together, be careful lest you fall in that very area?

It was a simple question with no malice intended. "Dave, when are you going to get around to raising funds for Marriage Alive?" Thirteen words brought up on Dave's mental computer all the conversations of twenty years about fund-raising. A lot of things in our work in marriage and family enrichment are fun, but not fund-raising; it's at the absolute bottom! We had beaten this issue to death in many conversations, but here it was again, poking up its ugly head! Could the authors follow their own advice? Not at the moment. We were definitely in Stage Two Communication, and the verbal bullets were flying. How could we resolve this issue and bury it once and for all? Was there any hope for resolution? Not until we took our own suggestions.

First, we had to put our "hot potato" down and let it cool. If we go head to head in confrontation, we lose perspective, attack each other, and generally make the situation—whatever it is—worse. This conflict really caught us off guard—especially after we had spent the day writing about good communication!

While our potato was cooling and our common sense was returning, we both became fearful—if this doesn't work for us, why are we writing about it? The fund-raising issue had been around for a long time, and we had resolved it before. Yet the rapid growth in our Marriage Alive ministry brought new funding needs. We decided to walk through the four steps of resolving honest conflict together. Our notes looked something like this:

STEPS FOR RESOLVING CONFLICT

Step One: Define the Problem

Neither of us enjoys or is gifted in fund-raising, yet funds must be raised for the ongoing ministry of Marriage Alive International (MAI).

What issues and unresolved conflicts lurk in the shadows of your marriage? Now is the time to choose one of them and go through this process with us. Let us encourage you to start with a simple one. Maybe you have progressed past the wet towels, but if finances are a "biggie," wait until you've practiced a little to tackle that one. For now, write down the problem you've decided to think about as we walk through these steps.

An issue we would like to resolve is:

_____

_____

Step Two: Identify Which of You Feels the Greater Need for a Solution and the Other Person's Contribution to the Problem.

We both needed a solution. Claudia possibly felt more insecure about the MAI financial situation than Dave did, but both admitted the need for a well-thought-through fund-raising plan. Both of us had contributed to the problem by doing very little to let others know of the need.

Look back at your problem. Which one of you needs a solution? Which one is contributing to the problem?

_____ feels the greatest need for a solution.

_____ is contributing to the problem.

Step Three: Suggest Alternate Solutions.

Our list went something like this:
1. Choose another line of work.
2. Dave assumes full responsibility for fund-raising.
3. Claudia assumes full responsibility for fund-raising.
4. Cut back on existing programs and ministry.

Now make your own list and be willing to brainstorm. Adding humor helps to relieve tension.

1. _____
2. _____
3. _____
4. _____
5. _____
6. _____

Step Four: Select a Plan of Action.

None of our alternative solutions was realistic. It was time to compromise. Both of us had a lot invested in our ministry and wanted to see it grow and expand. We needed to approach any possible solution as a team, yet the principle of who has the expertise didn't relate to the situation. We both were weak in this area. It didn't make the top ten in our "I'd like most to do" list—it wasn't on the list at all!

Here was our compromise agreement.

1. Claudia agreed to stop nagging and to help where she could. Specifically, she would help to edit letters and mailings.
2. Dave agreed to stop procrastinating and to do what he could do, rather than concentrating on what he couldn't do. He would work on improving communication with present contributors.
3. Both would monitor spending and look for ways to economize. In business, we have learned to add staff to supplement our weak areas, and that's just what we did. We recently added to our board of directors a key couple with expertise in administration and fund-raising. As our new director gives suggestions and advice, we follow up with action. We have learned an important principle—we do what we can, one thing at a time.

Is our financial crunch over? Far from it, but we are making progress—we are on the same team, and things are much more pleasant at the Arps'.

What is the solution to your problem? Look back at your list of alternatives. One might seem to be an obvious answer. Or, like the Arps, you might want to reject them all and devise a new plan. You may want to write your plan of action here.

Our plan of action is _____

_____

_____

_____

Everybody Has Problems

Life is not problem free. We are told in James 1:2–4, that we will have problems but that God will use them to teach us how to persevere. When we think of problems, we normally think, "Oh, no—I was just beginning to feel hopeful." God gives us a different perception when He tells us in James 1:12 and 1 Peter 1:7 that problems can actually produce hope and that biblical hope does not disappoint us!

As long as we are married or alive, we will face hard situations and have to make choices. The dullest marriages on earth are the ones where both spouses have decided to coexist and just tolerate one another. No conflict but no intimacy either. Let us challenge you to choose repeatedly to process your anger, frustrations, and differences and strive for intimacy. Your marriage is worth it!

A Word of Caution

Choose your timing wisely. Avoid trying to resolve conflict late at night when you're tired, and when you're hungry or already out of sorts. And remember, power plays destroy the relationship. Don't be like the workshop participant who really thought he was always right! It's hard to work together on resolution without pulling out emotional blackmail, but it really is worth all it takes to achieve honest resolution. Your marriage team will be stronger for it! And when it applies, remember our suggestion to look to the one with more expertise in an area.

One Last Illustration from the Arp Archives

Years ago when we were asked to move to Europe, it was on very short notice—six weeks! At the time we had

three very small children and were happily settled in Knoxville, Tennessee. God was blessing our ministry with growth
and expansion. Move? Who would even consider it? Dave
did. Claudia didn't. Here was an instant opportunity for conflict resolution!

We spent many long hours discussing the pros and cons
of such a drastic move. Dave saw the opportunities, adventure, and challenge of being in on the ground floor (really
the sub-basement) of a new work. Claudia saw giving up her
family, friends, and home that she loved and all the compli-
cations of moving and surviving in a foreign culture with
three small, active boys. Dave was challenged. Claudia was
scared. Time was running out.

We prayed together and separately about the possible
move. Dave got peace. Claudia got panic! Finally, the deadline drew near. Were we about to give up the opportunity of
a lifetime? There were no easy answers or solutions. Finally,
we each took time alone to pray and seek God's guidance. In
the end we made the move. Claudia capitulated.

"I'll never forget the feeling of being totally out of synch
with Dave. He felt so strongly about not passing up this opportunity. Finally I realized he felt stronger about us going
than I felt about us staying. Also I realized that his feelings
were based on how our gifts meshed with the job opportunity, coupled with a strong conviction that God was actually
calling us to Europe.

"My opinion was based on fear of the unknown and giving up what I did know. At that point, I made the decision for
good or evil, for richer or for poorer (where had I heard
those lines before?) to go along with his strong leading. After
all, if it didn't work out, we could always come home!

"Was it easy? You've got to be kidding! It was the hardest thing I ever did. I was sure we had made the biggest mis-
take of our lives. Did I immediately feel at home in
Germany? Are you serious? I got there physically in July,

and my emotions arrived in February! But in the end, I was glad I took the risk. We went for three years and we stayed almost ten. We now call those years the Golden Years. God blessed our ministry and our family."

Other times when Claudia has felt strongly about a decision, Dave has capitulated. It's not easy to discern God's leading. At times, we have done our best to make the right decisions, yet experienced disastrous results. Do we give up on resolving conflict and seeking to make wise team decisions? No! And neither should you!

What about when you reach a stalemate and you just can't seem to work things out? Remember, a professional counselor can give you short-term help. If you're going down a one-way street in the wrong direction, you don't need a pedestrian shouting to you that you're wrong. What you really need is a friendly policeman to come along, stop the traffic, and help you get turned around. That's what a counselor can do for your marriage.

One couple found our workshop did just that for them. "We've had lots of problems the past couple of years. A cross-country move and new baby added to our stress level," they told us. "This workshop helped to jump start our marriage. We are back on track. We know we still have issues to resolve and that we'll always have areas we need to work through, but now we have tools we can use to solve them and stay on track."

Our hope for you is that this chapter will help you do the same!

TRACKING TOGETHER

Getting Back On When You Jump Track

Purpose:
> To learn more appropriate ways of handling conflict
> To resolve one issue

Preparation:
> Review Chapter 9, "Getting Back On When You Jump
> Track"
> Fill out exercises and be ready to discuss

Our Tracking Time is:
> Date and Time _____
> Location _____

What needs to be done to make it happen:
> 1. _____
> 2. _____
> 3. _____

Tracking-together Time:
> 1. How Do You Handle Anger? (p. 151)
> 2. Areas That Trigger Conflict (p. 153)
> 3. Steps for Resolving Conflict (p. 158)

CHAPTER TEN

Building a Christian Marriage

J ust pray this prayer, commit your marriage to God, and everything will work out." The words of the Bible study leader were still ringing in Jill and Sam's ears as they drove home. They had prayed again at the meeting, as they had in the past, that God would heal their marriage, but their communication was as bad as ever. Why didn't God answer their prayers? Shouldn't being a Christian make a difference in the quality of their marriage relationship?

Yes, it should. But it doesn't happen automatically by just praying a prayer any more than a marriage ceremony assures us of a great sexual relationship. Please don't misunderstand us. Having a deep, abiding personal faith in God has greatly benefited our marriage relationship. But to be honest, a few times our Christian walk actually caused friction.

It wasn't until after we had children of our own that Christianity became a reality in our lives. As wonderful as our newfound faith was, it was not a panacea for all our problems. We remember stressful situations both before and after we discovered a vital faith in Jesus Christ. In other words, having Christ in our lives doesn't mean we automatically know and apply biblical principles to our marriage. It doesn't mean we will have a stress-free marriage—but the potential for improvement is there!

In the first years of our marriage, we had a great relationship even though our Christian faith was quite dormant. Relating to each other was easy for us. We were so "in love" that we felt secure. Sure, we had the usual disagreements, but we didn't experience any serious stress until our first son was born. Then reality began to hit us.

Just three weeks before our first child arrived we completed a move from Germany to Washington State (at the request of Uncle Sam). Stress was building even in our naturally wonderful marriage. A difficult birth and the added trauma of a baby who didn't breathe at first motivated Claudia to pray sincerely, "Please let this baby live, and we will do all we can to raise him in a Christian home!" God answered. He lived and is now a happily married attorney at law, but the in-between part, "raising him in a Christian home," just wasn't that simple.

After four years of marriage, we were used to our freedom and flexibility. Both came to an abrupt end when the first child arrived! Not only were our wings clipped, but we were totally exhausted. We had never really understood the ramifications of that little word *colic*. We got a quick education and had the bloodshot eyes to prove it!

For the first time we began to snap at each other. We weren't getting a very good start in establishing a Christian home. It seemed the harder we tried, the worse things got. Once in sheer desperation, Claudia left the apartment, got in the car, and drove around aimlessly for several hours. (You will appreciate that when you know that on Claudia's list of things she likes to do, driving is next to taking out the garbage or cleaning the bathroom!)

During this time, we were trying our best to stay on track in our marriage. Many long conversations brought us to the same basic conclusion—we were committed to each other and to our son, and we did desire to raise him in a Christian home. We just didn't know how.

Fast-forward with us a couple of years. Living in Atlanta, Georgia, and expecting our second child, we were still committed to having a Christian home, so we got involved in a church. We also renewed friendships with dear friends from our college days, and we began to piece together the elements of building a truly Christian home.

Seeds planted in our childhood began to take root. We both came to a new understanding of who Christ is, why He came to this earth, and what He personally did for us when He died on the cross. We accepted His offer of forgiveness for the past, eternal life for the future, and His daily personal involvement in our lives. As God began to be more real to us in our own personal lives, we began to experience His presence in our home.

Initially this was an "up" time in our lives and in our marriage—as if we had been plugged into a new power source. Finding our security and significance as individuals in our relationship with a living, loving, and caring God freed us to love and accept each other.

From this point it was smooth sailing. Right? Wrong! We sailed right into another time of incredible stress. Two children were even more confining than one. Dave's job as a marketing representative with IBM required quite a bit of travel, and our new faith, though wonderful, wasn't helping our communication. Claudia filled her free time with Bible studies, new Christian friends, and other activities. Dave, who had little discretionary time, resented her enthusiasm for all these "Christian" activities and felt ignored. To be honest, trying to live out our Christianity was complicating our lives, and things were getting worse, not better!

Consider two other couples. Dick and Sally, a Christian

couple, were active in the church and appeared to have a deep abiding faith in the Lord. Dick was a deacon and worked with the youth group. Sally was involved in the women's program. Most people assumed they had a great marriage. But, without a word, Dick left his wife and family.

How could a couple love God with all their hearts, base their lives on their Christian faith, yet experience marriage derailment? Christian marriages should be the most stable marriages around. Knowing Christ personally should make a difference!

The second couple, Jim and Sherry, had little interest in spiritual matters, but had a great marriage relationship. We met this couple in Vienna, Austria, where Jim held a high position in his country's embassy. Sherry was a freelance writer and active in the community. They were both involved with each other and with their children. Although in a high-pressure environment, Jim and Sherry made their marriage and family a high priority. God really didn't play an active role in their daily lives. But their marriage seemed to be alive and growing; their children, happy and well adjusted. They were fun to be around and could have written the script for the "Cosby" show.

Wait. Didn't someone mess up the script or juggle the couples? Shouldn't Dick and Sally have the growing marriage and Jim and Sherry be the statistic? For years we have puzzled over marriages that function great outside the church and marriages that barely hang on within the church. But as we looked closer, we began to understand. A marriage of two Christians doesn't automatically make a Christian marriage.

We don't have to look very deeply today to see statistics that Christian marriages are breaking up in great numbers, and sadly those numbers include Christian leaders and pastors. In some churches divorce seems epidemic. Recently a pastor commented to us that he spends most of his time counseling couples and trying to help keep their marriages intact.

In Chapter 1 we talked about the fact that biblical principles for building positive relationships work! But only if you use them and apply them to your marriage. Jim and Sherry unknowingly were tapping into solid, healthy, biblical principles for building positive relationships, so they built an alive, functioning, growing marriage. Dick and Sally, although they loved God and were trying to serve and honor Him, were not applying those biblical principles.

Let's go back to our situation in Atlanta as we struggled to integrate our newfound faith into our marriage. We had become so involved in our Christian activities (or at least Claudia had) that our time for each other was sketchy and shallow, but we were determined to do something about it. We wanted to get back on track. We wanted to have a Christian marriage. But just what made a marriage uniquely Christian?

What Is a "Christian" Marriage?

A Christian marriage involves three—the husband, the wife, and God. As we grew individually in our relationship with God, we also grew closer together. First, we realized that we were each responsible to God for our individual relationship with Him. But as we grew closer to God, our tracks moved closer together and gave us a common focus in life. Consider the following diagram.

Dave was on one side and Claudia was on the other, and God was at the top. As we grew closer to God, we grew closer to each other. An enriched, healthy, Christian marriage team involves three. Do you remember the cord of three strands in Chapter 1? It's much stronger than a two-cord strand. Our relationship with God strengthens a Christian marriage. Personally we discovered that "a cord of three strands is not easily broken."

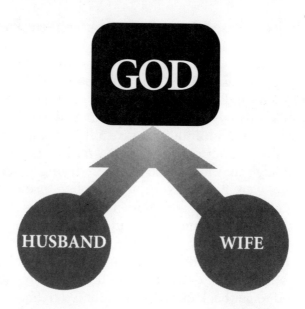

Christian Marriage—A New Way of Communicating

Another unique resource in a Christian marriage is prayer. God delights in the praise and prayers of His people and tells us if we lack wisdom to ask and He will give it liberally to us (James 1:5).

We began the habit of praying together, which we have continued over the years. Sometimes it's easy. Other times it's hard. When our relationship with each other is not running smoothly, it's difficult, if not impossible, for us to pray together. Sometimes we could only pray, "Lord, help us to get back on track so we can pray together!" Amazingly, He answered that prayer.

Another hindrance to praying together was that one of us was more verbal than the other and could "out pray" the other. We discovered if we first made a list of things we wanted to pray about and took turns praying, we concentrated on communicating with God, not trying to impress one another.

Are you in the habit of praying together? Maybe like us, you are hesitant, shy, or reserved. Or maybe you'd like to pray together but just don't know how to get started. Why not take a few minutes right now and make a start? You may want to list things you'd like to commit to the Lord in prayer. For instance, maybe you are struggling with finances or dealing with a strong-willed child. Perhaps you've been hesitant to share with your mate how you really feel about things. Whatever concerns you, pray about it together.

MAKING A MARRIAGE PRAYER LIST

I want us to pray about:

1. _____

2. _____

3. _____

4. _____

A word of caution: Don't use prayer for attacking your mate. If you're just beginning to pray together, don't start with the most tense situation, like the mate who prayed, "Lord, please help my mate to understand and meet my sexual needs."

A Christian Marriage Follows the Teachings of Christ

When we began to establish a prayer life together, we also began to study the Scriptures to learn what Jesus taught about relationships. Apart from the principles of leaving, cleaving, and becoming one flesh, Jesus had little to say directly about the husband-wife relationship, but He did lay down principles for living that may be applied to all human relationships.

When asked what was the greatest commandment of all, Jesus replied, "Love the LORD your God with all your heart, with all your soul, with all your mind, and with all your strength. . . . Love your neighbor as yourself. There is no commandment greater than these" (Mark 12:30–31).

At the human level, the key word is *neighbor*. In the Old Testament, *neighbor* can mean fellow countryman, dweller, friend, or inhabitant. But in the New Testament, *neighbor* means the person closest to you. And for any married person that is the marriage partner, the one chosen to share life at its deepest and most intimate level. If we love our marriage partner as we love ourselves, we will have his or her best interests at heart, we will want to serve, not be served, and we will resist the urge to manipulate or pull power plays. We will have a relationship based on love and trust. We will also fulfill the original promise in Genesis 2—that God gave Adam and Eve to each other because each needed, above all else, a companion.

Not only did Jesus have much to say about building positive relationships, but He also modeled those principles. His life on this planet demonstrated love in action. So many times marital conflict would be resolved if we followed the example of Christ. Too often we are "me" centered and want things to work out "my" way. Christ taught just the opposite approach. Consider some of the ways Jesus modeled the essence of positive relationships.

Christian Marriage—A New Way of Serving

Jesus said that the first shall be last and the last shall be first, that we should choose to give rather than to re-

ceive. Our marriage relationships would be revolution-
ized if we approached marriage as servants. Jesus washed
the disciples' feet. We just want someone to wash the
dishes.

It's hard to learn to serve each other, especially in the
closeness of a marriage relationship. We never have
functioned very well in our marriage when one or the other
has to travel. It was especially hard when our children were
small and Dave traveled a lot. He would come home exhausted and tired of people. One such time still stands out
in our memory. He was selling data processing services
to small-to-medium-sized companies and had worked for
months with one particular company. At the last minute,
when the company was actually supposed to sign the contract, it reneged, and Dave came home empty-handed—all
ready to jump into his shell and hibernate.

Claudia, on the other hand, had been at home with two
preschoolers. The older had just shared the chicken pox
with the younger, and Claudia was "itching" to get out of the
house and have some adult conversation.

We were both so caught up in our own miseries that we
didn't serve one another. We had to regroup, apologize, and
start over again. To be honest, years later, we still get caught
in the web of "my needs" and "your needs." Knowing the
principle doesn't mean we always apply it. But that is our
goal, and sometimes we remember!

Why not make a list of ways you can serve your mate
today (like being sensitive to your mate's mood)? If Claudia
had not crowded Dave when he came home discouraged
from his business trip, things could have gone differently. Or
maybe you could give up what you want to do for your mate.
For example, Dave could have gone the extra "servant mile"
and taken Claudia out for a couple of hours before withdrawing into his shell.

SERVING ONE ANOTHER

I can serve my mate by:

1. _____

2. _____

3. _____

Christian Marriage—A New Way of Loving

In a Christian marriage not only are we to serve one another, but we are to love one another unconditionally. Christ loves us not "if" or "because" we do or don't do certain things. He loves us "in spite of" what we do or don't do. We should love our mate the same way!

If you want to see if you are loving your mate unconditionally, read through 1 Corinthians 13 and substitute your name for "love." Here are several verses to get you started: "_____ is patient, _____ is kind. _____ does not envy; _____ does not boast, is not proud. _____ is not rude, _____ is not self-seeking, _____ is not easily angered, _____ keeps no record of wrongs. _____ does not delight in evil but rejoices with the truth. _____ always protects, _____ always trusts, _____ always hopes, _____ always perseveres" (NIV).

How did you do? Not so well? You may be thinking that you just can't do that. And you're right. Jesus models a supernatural kind of love. He alone can give us the power to love our mates in this way. On the other hand, we need to realize that love is a choice we can make. Too often, if we don't feel loving, we think that love has died. A German doctor, Dr. Arne Hoffman, told us that the biochemical phase of love is sometimes over in as little as three months after the ceremony. Unconditional love is much more than a romantic, tingly feeling. Tingles come and go, but real love manifests itself in the trenches of life.

Sometimes we give each other unconditional love in the hard times—when Dave's migraine headache just wouldn't go away and we had to cancel our dinner out with friends and Claudia resisted the urge to complain, or when Claudia had a root canal and the dentist said, "Take a couple of aspirin when you get home and you'll be just fine." Who was he kidding? Not Claudia, whose tolerance level for pain is slightly above zero. Through the throbbing pain that night she appreciated Dave's ice packs, Jell-O™, and gentleness. In other times and other situations, our unconditional love hasn't been that unconditional, but sometimes we do follow the example of Christ. Let us challenge you to let Jesus be your model and help you put love into action.

Christian Marriage—A Deeper Acceptance

Jesus is our model of how we are to accept each other. Picture this scenario. Jesus, the Son of God, is about to be baptized. Whom does He choose for this great honor? A weird-looking character named John the Baptist. If we had been Jesus, we would have requested that John get some decent clothes for the occasion and visit the local hairdresser. Unlike us, Jesus had the ability to look at the heart, not the appearance.

Are we accepting our mates? Do we often react to surface issues? Claudia will never forget one summer when she decided to get her hair cut—we're talking really cut. It was even shorter than Claudia had expected, and Dave's nonaccepting comment, "It makes you look older, doesn't it?" definitely made Claudia look more angry!

It's not always easy to accept that extra ten pounds you wish your mate would lose or having to live on a restrictive budget or the little irritating habit that won't go away. A starting point to deeper acceptance might be to list ways you know deep down inside you need to accept your mate. This is a personal exercise for you, not to be shared with your mate.

ACCEPTING EACH OTHER

Things I need to accept about my mate are:

1. _____

2. _____

3. _____

Being a Christian doesn't give you instant marital success. As Christ demonstrated, relationships take time and work. Let's go back to our two couples. Maybe you, like Dick and Sally, really love God and desire to serve and honor Him, but your marriage relationship is a struggle. Or maybe you identify with Jim and Sherry. You have a workable, growing marriage relationship, but you wonder if there isn't more.

After we moved back to the States, we kept up with Jim and Sherry for several years. While their marriage remained intact, their situation changed drastically. Jim was part of the fallout of reshuffling at his country's embassy, and he spent almost two years job hunting. At this time the "good life" was not so good to them. When we lived in Vienna, we talked several times with Jim and Sherry about our faith in Christ, and while interest was not too high at that point, we have often wondered if perhaps circumstances have increased their interest in spiritual things. There are no atheists in foxholes.

Where do you turn when you are in the foxholes of your marriage? This is the place that our Christian faith has really made a difference.

One Foxhole Experience

The day started no differently from any other day, but our lives would never quite be the same again. Dave called to say that he would be a couple of hours late, but gave no explanation. Claudia assumed another big project had come up at work, but Dave's story was something completely different!

Claudia knew he had been frustrated in his job but wasn't prepared for his announcement, "Honey, I quit!"

"But how are we going to live?" was Claudia's immediate response. We had two sons, a house payment, and a meager savings account.

"I'm really not sure," Dave responded. "But you know I've been dissatisfied at work. Well, I prayed about it. I prayed that the company would let me transfer to another division, but it didn't work out, so I assumed God was leading me to another job somewhere else."

"Did you ever consider," Claudia interjected, "that He might want you to keep your present job while you looked for another one?"

If you have ever gone through a job change (by choice or otherwise) you know that fear in the pit of your stomach, which privately tells you, "I might starve to death." If our Christian faith could really make a difference in our marriage and lives, here was the acid test!

Here are the differences as we remember them many years later. First we were able to commit our situation to God and pray about it. That third cord in our three strands held firm and steady even though our two cords were wobbly. When we became fearful about the unknown future, we acknowledged that God was with us in this adventure and would continue to lead and care for us.

Secondly, we found our identity and significance as individuals in who we were in Christ. This gave us a real sense of security. Claudia was not just "the wife of an unemployed husband," and Dave wasn't just "the husband of an insecure, somewhat frightened wife!" We were both children of God, and we sensed He had a purpose for our lives. Finding our security in our relationship with the Lord, we were able to accept each other and pull together and not apart. With God's help we tried to support one another.

Another job did come along—one much better suited to Dave's talents and abilities and one that eventually led us to our work together in marriage and family enrichment. This wasn't an easy time in our lives; we would not like to repeat it. But in thinking about this situation twenty-something years later, we're able to see how our Christian faith allowed us to stretch and take the risk, to step out of our comfort zone and to do it together.

Does knowing Christ make a difference? In *The Sacred Fire* Drs. David and Vera Mace say: "What the New Testament makes possible for a man, a woman, or a married couple is an encounter with Jesus of Nazareth. Therefore, it is only those who have encountered the ever-living Christ and have surrendered their lives to Him who will surely know how to make their marriages truly Christian."[1]

Christ demonstrated how to live, and He will empower

us to express love, to be sensitive to the needs of another, to be open and honest, to act considerately and unselfishly, to deal with anger and conflict, to forgive and be reconciled, and to reflect God's love in our love for each other. When we incorporate these qualities into our lives, they will make our marriages truly Christian!

Having an Intentional Marriage

Let us encourage you to take some time right now to reflect on where you are in your marriage and in your spiritual pilgrimage and in which direction you want to move. Discovering where you are and where you want to go in your marriage relationship can be exciting. Now is a good time to look back to Chapter 6 and review the goals you have already set for your marriage track. You may want to adjust or expand your goals and include new ideas and insights you have gained from Part 2.

To pull it all together, we suggest writing out your very own Declaration of Intention, a general statement of the goals you want to achieve as a couple. Businesses and organizations spend immense amounts of time to come up with a mission statement—the essence of what they want to accomplish. Your Declaration of Intention is the mission statement for your marriage.

You can make it as simple or elaborate as you want. The key is that you both agree with your final statement. In our Marriage Alive Workshop, couples write out their Declaration of Intention for their marriage as a contract of what they both want to see happen. Usually we don't see what the couples come up with, but recently a couple shared theirs with us. It was so creative that we asked permission to share it with you. Since commitment is so central to the marriage relationship, they wrote an acrostic using the word *commitment*.

OUR DECLARATION OF INTENTION

C—Christ centered relationship

O—Openness in our communication

M—Maintain awareness of the state of our relationship

M—Mount full-scale war against the one who would tear us apart—not each other

I—Intentional in the application of skills learned

T—Team work is our goal—both of us are necessary, therefore both have valuable input

M—Model for our children and others the teaching of Christ

E—Encourage each other in maintaining an eternal perspective

N—Nurture each other, spiritually, physically, emotionally

T—Train for the road before us, trust one another, train up our children in the way they should go

Personally Applied

One of the great benefits of our work in marriage enrichment over the years is that it has motivated us to continue to work at having our own "intentional marriage." As you have probably gleaned from the pages of *The Marriage Track*, our marriage is in process, hopefully in the direction of growth. The argument we had after completing the chapter on communication was not intentional! But we continue to work at the task of building a positive, healthy Christian marriage—to work at keeping our marriage on track.

As we have compiled the many exercises in this book or as we lead another Marriage Alive Workshop, we continue to benefit from the exercises personally. Please do not consider *The Marriage Track* a one-time experience. We know couples who have a yearly checkup when they repeat all the exercises in this book. In the same vein, we keep our own personal Marriage Declaration of Intention in a somewhat fluid state, ever looking for better ways to express the intentions of our marriage. As of our last edit, here is our Declaration of Intention. We hope it will encourage you to dig deep to find your own unique statement of your marriage.

DECLARATION OF INTENTION

As a couple we are committed to the pursuit of the following goals for our marriage team:

- A commitment to growth by regularly setting goals and objectives for our marriage
- A commitment to communicate our true feelings, to build up and encourage each other, and to process and work through anger and conflict situations
- A commitment to find space in our togetherness and unity in our diversity and to continue to grow as individuals
- A commitment to strive to be a model for our own children and for others of the outworking of the teachings of Christ about creative love in close relationships

WRITING OUR DECLARATION OF INTENTION

Now write out your Declaration of Intention. Take plenty of time and work together until you are both satisfied with the wording and content.

DECLARATION OF INTENTION

_____

_____

_____

_____

_____

_____

Signed: _____   _____

Date: _____

Christian Marriage—A Lighthouse

Chuck Colsen, in *Kingdoms in Conflict,* talks about the church's having little Christian outposts in a world that desperately needs hope. Our marriages and families should be little platoons that give light to others and create a thirst for growing, healthy marriage and family relationships.

Your marriage can be a lighthouse to a hurting and confused world. Today we need a widespread movement that will produce large numbers of Christian marriages that provide working models of Jesus' teachings about creative love in human relationships. Wouldn't you like to be a part is seeing this happen?

Start Your Own Lighthouse Group

If you put one log by itself, the flame may go dim, but several logs together burn brightly. Over the years other couples have helped us stay on track, like our dear friends, David and Vera Mace, who have supported us and modeled how to have a positive and growing Christian marriage. Let us encourage you to get involved with a small group of couples who are committed to marital growth. If you want to start your own marriage growth group, there is a Leader's Guide to go with *The Marriage Track*. For more information about these resources contact

Marriage Alive International, Inc.,
P.O. Box 90303,
Knoxville, TN 37990

Another suggestion is to join A.C.M.E. The Association of Couples in Marriage Enrichment was established in 1973 by David and Vera Mace and is a network of couples working for better marriages. A.C.M.E. activities and resources focus on prevention and growth and include weekend retreats, local marriage growth groups, and a practical bimonthly newsletter. Let us encourage you to become a member of A.C.M.E. You'll have the opportunity to experience new growth in your marriage. For more information, contact:

A.C.M.E.
502 North Broad Street
P.O. Box 10596
Winston-Salem, NC 27108
800-634-8325

Have Fun Along the Way!

Our marriage has been enriched by our ability to laugh and play together. Laughter dispels tension and is physically healthy for the body! It's also like a vitamin for the soul!

We asked a friend what he remembered about his parents—what special heritage they passed down to him that had enriched his marriage and family life. He thought for a moment and said, "There are two things that stand out in my mind. At first they didn't seem to be related, but the more I think about it, they really are. One—I remember my parents praying together. Whatever hard situations we were facing in our family, we prayed about it. The second thing I remember is hearing my parents roaring with laughter. They made sure that they had fun together as a couple and with us as a family."

We hope this chapter has encouraged you to pray together and make your marriage truly a Christian marriage. The next section of *The Marriage Track* is intended to help you have fun and laugh together. We have designed ten dates for mates to help you have fun tracking on your own. Let us encourage you to have dates, to talk, to play, and to laugh.

An enriched, fun-loving Christian marriage can make a difference in our quality of life. We can stay on track and leave the heritage of a positive marriage track for our offspring and their spouses to follow. Take the advice of many who returned from the Gulf War. In their foxholes, they had the time to evaluate their lives and make some decisions about what is really of value. They said, "I'm going to spend time with my wife/husband/family. . . . My faith in God has been strengthened. . . . I'm going to work harder on my marriage. . . . Relationships are what is really important. . . . I just want to be with those I love."

How about you? You don't have to wait until another war or until a crisis. Now is the time to build the relationship with your mate. Now is the time to establish a truly Christian marriage. Now is the time to get your marriage on track!

TRACKING TOGETHER

Building a Christian Marriage

Purpose:
 To consider how faith in God relates to marriage
 To look at the teachings and examples of Jesus in
  building close, loving relationships
 To have an intentional marriage

Preparation:
 Review Chapter 10, "Building a Christian Marriage"
 Fill out exercises and be ready to discuss

Our Tracking Time is:
 Date and Time _____
 Location _____

What needs to be done to make it happen:
 1. _____
 2. _____
 3. _____

Tracking-together Time:
 Together discuss the following exercises:
 1. Making a Marriage Prayer List (p. 171)
 2. Serving One Another (p. 174)
 3. Accepting Each Other (p. 176)
 4. Writing Our Declaration of Intention (p. 181)

PART THREE

TRACKING ON YOUR OWN

CHAPTER ELEVEN

Ten Dates for Mates

Recently we were with two couples who are a lot of fun. Both are committed to their marriages and families. *What a great opportunity,* we thought, *to do a little research on dating your mate.* So we asked, "What has been your most fun date?"

One mate said, "You mean before we got married?" That was not exactly what we had in mind. The other couple told us about their attempted big date. They went to a nice local hotel for an extravagant getaway and ended up in a room by the ice machine where a college fraternity party was setting a record for noise production. It was so loud that in the middle of the night they packed up, checked out, and went back to their relatively quiet home—that's relative if you want to compare three preschoolers with a fraternity party.

It wasn't that our friends hadn't tried to date their mates, but both couples confessed that outside of dates to soccer, baseball games, and swim meets, they had actually done very little dating in the past few years. So even though our friends have growing, healthy marriages, they couldn't help us with resources for this section of *The Marriage Track*. Instead they needed this chapter!

For the last ten chapters we have given you some simple, but meaty exercises to help you keep your relationship headed in the right direction. In this final chapter, we want to give you some fun things you can do to enjoy the adventure! Unlike the other chapters in *The Marriage Track*, this one doesn't require following a correct order. Simply choose the dates that sound fun to you, schedule them, and go for it. As interruptions come along, simply reschedule.

If you are the more methodical type of couple you might consider having one fun date between each chapter of this book. However you approach the subject of dating your mate, let us encourage you to carry through. It will be the icing on the cake!

Following are ten of the Arp's favorite dates. You can use our date suggestions to get started. They are seed ideas; it's up to you and your creativity to plant them in your marriage and harvest a crop of good times together.

1. Walk and Talk Date

The Walk and Talk Date is one of our favorites and one we actually do several times each week. For us, it started years ago. Whenever we went to the beach, we loved to walk on the beach and talk each morning and again at sunset. But once home and back to the regular grind, we forgot all about walking, until Claudia suffered a back injury and began to walk as part of her recovery therapy. That was two years ago and we are still walking!

Let us tell you why this date is so popular with us. First, it fits our budget! Now that we walk regularly, we have invested in walking shoes, but no special equipment is really needed. Second, it's so simple. We are the spontaneous type and this date requires no preplanning. (If you have small children, you may need to get a baby sitter or coordinate your own schedules.)

Often we have a Walk and Talk Date after dinner in the evening. We recently read that walking after a meal speeds up digestion by 50 percent, which brings up another benefit of this date—it's good for your health!

Where to Walk?

You can walk anywhere you want to. Often we walk around our neighborhood block, approximately half a mile. If we walk around the block for thirty minutes at our speed, we have walked about two miles. The speed you walk is only relevant if you are doing it for physical fitness—another benefit of this date.

Other places we like to walk are:

- A local exercise trail
- Around the track at a local high school
- In other neighborhoods
- In shopping malls (Some malls open early to accommodate local walkers. It's a great time to go. No stores are open so you don't spend any money.)
- A mountain trail (We recently walked eight miles up to a mountain lodge in the Smokey Mountains, spent the night, and walked back the next day. This extended walking date obviously requires preplanning.)
- Through the old part of town
- On special bike and walking paths
- And, of course, the beach!

Others Tips for Walking Dates

If there are loose dogs in your neighborhood or wherever you are walking, take along a stick. Claudia, who was bitten by a dog as a child, is skeptical of any unknown dog. Dave continually kids her, "There's the dog that got the fax that Claudia would be walking on this road!" For Claudia, dogs are a good reason to walk in "twos."

Leave your Walkman™ at home. In our neighborhood there is a couple who walk together—sort of. They both listen to portable recorders as they walk. For us this defeats the main purpose of walking together: an opportunity to talk privately with each other.

Take along an index card and pencil. We use this time to brainstorm, and if we don't write down our great ideas, by the time we get home, we've forgotten them!

Sometimes we pick a topic to discuss before we start our Walk and Talk Date.

Lastly, have fun. You'll find that walking and talking will help keep your marriage on track!

2. Have a Surprise Date

Our friends, Nancy and Paul, really pulled this one off in grand fashion—or to be more correct, Nancy did! Paul is a cardiologist and has a very busy medical practice. Since they have three teenagers, dating time is hard to find. Nancy decided to do something about it.

Completely unknown to Paul, she arranged for a young couple, who work with a local youth group, to spend a week with their adolescents. One of Paul's favorite things that he rarely is able to do is to go snorkeling, so Nancy decided to plan a week away in the Bahamas. She coordinated with Paul's office and had them clear his schedule for a week. To keep Paul "in the dark" his secretary wrote in fictitious appointments for an entire week.

Imagine Paul's astonishment when he went to work on Monday morning to find the waiting room empty except for his wife—with plane tickets and suitcase in hand. She whisked him off to the Bahamas for a week of snorkeling and fun!

Now, for most of us, this would be a once-in-a-lifetime date if we could pull it off at all. You may not be able to fly to the Bahamas, but the idea of a Surprise Date can be realized on any scale or budget.

Remember when Dave kidnapped Claudia to the Vienna Woods? (It was much more economical than a snorkeling date in the Bahamas—but, for us, just as much fun.)

Surprise Dates can be even simpler. On one particular Saturday, Claudia had been working hard to meet a writing deadline. About noon, Dave poked his head into the office and said, "Honey, be ready at seven tonight—we have a date!"

"Where are we going?" Claudia asked, surprised that they were going anywhere.

Imagine her surprise when Dave replied, "That's for me to know and you to find out. We're having a Surprise Date. Just be ready at seven!"

The element of surprise added a new dimension to our day. Just knowing Dave had taken the initiative to plan a surprise date gave Claudia a real boost in the middle of trying to meet a deadline. Dave enjoyed seeing Claudia mull over the question, "Just what is that guy up to now?"

Actually, the surprise element was the most fun part of the date. What kind of exotic place did we go? We went to a local cinema and saw a movie we had talked about seeing for months. (Our procrastination saved us money as it was now at the dollar theater!) The total cost of our surprise date was two dollars plus popcorn and drinks! Much cheaper than the Bahamas, but a Surprise Date just the same!

Other Surprise Date suggestions are:

- Dinner out or even just dessert and coffee
- A drive in the mountains

- A visit to a museum or art exhibit
- Window shopping—especially good when the stores are closed
- Visit a video store and pick out a favorite movie.
- Use your imagination and have fun surprising your mate.

You never know where the tracks might take you!

3. Have a Love Date

Recently we read an article with which we strongly disagree. Basically the article implied that Christian marriages may not be as sexually exciting because a Christian stays married to the same partner for so many years. We'd like to suggest that boredom—not having the same partner—is what makes sex mundane and blah. So to combat boredom in your love life, why not have a Love Date?

To break the monotony, plan a date and make love to each other some place you have never made love before. One couple took our suggestion and made love on their dining room table. Unfortunately, the table wasn't very sturdy and it fell in. Next time they said they would try their date under the table!

We had one of our favorite Love Dates in the early years of our marriage. We don't want to get into specifics, but we will tell you Claudia's dad was an apple grower and that a favorite song of ours is "Don't Sit Under the Apple Tree with Anyone Else but Me." An outside Love Date can be exhilarating, but in today's world please make sure you are in a private, secure, and safe place!

Here are some Love Date ideas:

- Rent a boat and find a secluded cove on a lake.
- Borrow the home of a friend who is out of town. (Once

we did just that. Our friends were the romantic type and had mirrors on their ceiling. That's not how we would choose to decorate our own bedroom, but it did make for an interesting date!)

- Find out which local hotels or motels have jacuzzies and take advantage of your research. Take along a basket of goodies to eat.
- Choose a different setting in your own home.
- Revisit the place you went on your honeymoon. (We can't do this because the place we went has been torn down.)
- Use your creativity and design your own Love Date.

We've been married thirty years (to the same person), and we have found that loving each other is more fulfilling and wonderful as the years go by—especially on Love Dates!

4. Milestones of a Marriage Date

What are some of the milestones of your marriage? Maybe you remembered some of them in Chapter 2 when you walked down memory lane. A milestone is any special event or situation that influenced the direction of your lives together. For us, our move to Europe was a milestone. Our marriage today is stronger because we were forced to deal with cracks in our marriage that probably would have gone undetected and unresolved had we remained in our former situation. Other milestones for us were deciding to start our family and beginning the practice of our "Monday Mornings" alone together.

We were aware that we had made choices, but never realized their significance in our lives until we had a Milestones of Our Marriage Date. We chose an evening when we were not rushed and went to a quiet restaurant for dinner.

We took along paper and pen and jumped back into history. We actually started with our first date and began to write down memories that were significant to either of us. Often we remembered different aspects of the events. One of the nicest things about this date is that our memories are uniquely ours and no one else's and create an intimacy reserved for just us two.

All you need for a Milestone of Your Marriage Date is:

- A few hours alone together (If you don't get all the way through your milestones, simply continue on your next Milestone Date.)
- Paper and pen to record your memories
- Your undivided attention on each other and your unique history

You'll be glad you took the time to remember and to focus on what is so important to both of you.

5. Have a Twenty-Four-Hour-Getaway Date

We have already told you about our weekend in Alabama (which should be listed under the Love Date). Since then we've taken many twenty-four-hour getaways by tacking twenty-four hours on to work travel and carving out some just-for-two time. When our children were young, twenty-four-hour getaways were a wonderful break from our parenting responsibilities and hassles at home and gave us time to focus on each other.

There is one Twenty-Four-Hour-Getaway Date we'll never forget! We were living in Germany and had discovered a wonderful farmhouse in the Black Forest. Our room came complete with a featherbed and a balcony overlooking the cattle grazing in the meadow and the mountains in the background. When we go away for our Twenty-Four-Hour-

Getaway Dates, we sometimes take off our watches and forget about the time. (Easy for Dave, hard for Claudia, but relaxing for both of us.) This was one of those times. Later that evening, we went to a small out-of-the-way German restaurant for dinner and talked and talked and talked. Time slipped by unnoticed until we began to get sleepy. Then thoughts of our cosy room in the farmhouse filled us with a warm feeling. We were so glad we had taken this time to be together.

The drive back to the farmhouse was uneventful. Then we made a discovery that would drastically change our romantic date. Our room key would not open the outside door! The farmer and his whole family had gone to bed, and we couldn't wake anyone up to open the door for us. Our romantic room was so close yet so far away! Fortunately we had a Volkswagen camper and were able to pull out the bed and sleep in it.

The next morning we got back into the farmhouse and into the room that we had inadvertently "missed" the night before. The moral of this story is if you go to a farmhouse or the equivalent, be sure to get a key that opens the outside door!

Other places you might consider for a Twenty-Four-Hour-Getaway Date are:

- Camping. (Not our choice, but good friends tell us it's great!)
- Again, you could swap homes with friends with one catch—they bring their kids to your house and keep yours too! You can do the same for your friends at another time.
- One couple we know rented a rustic cabin on a white-water stream in the North Georgia mountains.
- In the past generous friends have loaned us their beach condo.

• Don't overlook all the wonderful bed and breakfast inns.

The fall our nest emptied, we expanded our Twenty-Four-Hour-Getaway Date and spent several days touring bed and breakfasts in New England. We had a wonderful week, partly because in the years before the empty nest we had taken the time and made the effort to have Twenty-Four-Hour-Getaway Dates. Don't wait until you have the time and money or until the kids grow up—now is the time to make a track to your own special just-for-two getaway. Take it from us—you'll be glad you did!

6. Have a Sports Date

Our friends, Don and Betsy, set the pace when it comes to Sports Dates. In their late fifties they took up golf. Their empty nest had refilled again with offspring and grandchildren. Once again Betsy was driving carpools, and she and Don were finding time alone hard to come by. They weren't thrilled with their situation, so they decided to do something about it. They took up golf.

Don had played golf years before, but it was a totally new sport for Betsy. Their goal for their golf dates was to spend time together rather than to compete, so they set some unusual ground rules. They never kept score or even counted their strokes! They loved being outside and away from their refilled nest at home. Bill enjoyed encouraging Betsy, and after a few lessons and lots of practice, Betsy caught on to the game. Bill tells us that if they were to keep score, he's not sure who would win. We told him that it sounded to us like they were both winners.

What about you? Have you been neglecting a sport you love? Do you have a secret desire to learn a new sport. Why not get together with your mate and discuss sports you might like to pursue together? Consider the following:

- Golf
- Tennis
- Bowling
- Badmitten
- Fishing
- Hiking
- Chess (Some people consider board games quite sporting.)
- Swimming

Over the years we have benefited from our tennis dates. As we have already told you, we are not world-class players but do enjoy the game. While we are too competitive to ignore keeping score, we know one young married couple who, like Don and Betsy on the golf course, play tennis for hours and are happy just hitting the ball. They have played together so much that they are quite good. Recently we played doubles with them. We had to teach them the rules and how to keep score, but we also had to work hard to win a few games.

When we concentrate on spending time together, when we have Sports Dates with our mates, it's hard to lose!

7. Remember (If You Dare) All Your Anniversaries

When we suggested this date to our friends, Herb and Cary, their response was, "I don't think we would remember them!" Cary did say that they enjoyed setting aside date time to look at their wedding photos and wedding videos. (The latter is definitely for those married fewer years than us. There were no video recorders when we got married; our wedding pictures are even black and white!)

Your memories of your wedding day are an excellent beginning for this date. Don't worry if you can't remember every single anniversary. Sometimes memory is kind to us—some anniversaries may be better not remembered. On our first anniversary we were still in college and were moving from Atlanta to Athens, Georgia, so Claudia could go back to school. We borrowed Claudia's dad's apple truck. We'll never forget driving down a main street in Atlanta and realizing that our mattress has just fallen off the truck and was lying in the middle of a bridge. We stopped, ran to the bridge, and picked up our mattress. Not exactly the way we had pictured celebrating our first anniversary.

We spent our second anniversary in Germany at the invitation of Uncle Sam. Claudia had just arrived and Dave took her to a very special German restaurant. Sadly, our anniversary fell on Monday, and in Germany at that time all restaurants in our village were closed on Mondays!

If you had some anniversary flops, don't avoid this date. On our Remembering our Anniversaries Date, once we got past the first two (which we could even laugh about years later), we went on and shared a special time of remembering.

You may want to take paper and pen along on this date and record your memories—before, like our friends Herb and Cary, you forget them!

8. Have a Bike Date

Recently, someone told us you never forget how to ride a bike. Claudia wasn't really sure about that. It had been at least fifteen years since our last Bike Date, and she wasn't sure she really would remember how! We used to ride bikes by the Danube River in Vienna, Austria—but that was in our younger days! Our bikes had been sold long ago in a garage sale, but that didn't stop Dave from encouraging Claudia to have one more Biking-for-Two Date.

We're both glad we did and highly recommend this date to anyone who is brave enough to try it. We rented two bikes for several hours for a total cost of $4.50. We biked through a nature preserve, and when we got tired, we stopped and observed the wild horses, birds, and other wildlife. We had driven the same path the day before, and our perspective was amazingly different from a bike.

Let us encourage you to consider a Bike Date. If you enjoy it as much as we did, you can check out garage sales and look for two bikes to purchase. You even may be lucky enough to find two bike helmets, which will add to the safety of this date. If you really want to be daring, try a tandem bike for two. We aren't that brave yet, but you never know about next time!

9. Have a Prayer Date

Over the years, setting aside time to pray together has definitely brought our tracks closer together. We especially remember a Prayer Date in Vienna, Austria. It was during the time we were trying to discern God's leading for our future and whether we should move back to the States.

Our three children were in school, so we set a whole day aside for our Prayer Date. Our day was not very structured, but the things we did (and still remember) that were really meaningful were:

- Reading the Scriptures together
- Talking about how God had led us in the past and about answered prayers we had observed

- Writing down specific prayer requests
- Going out for lunch together and talking about our future
- Making a list of things we wanted to pray for each other and for each of our children for the next year (We made duplicates to tuck in each of our Bibles.)
- And most importantly, actually praying together

We completed our Prayer Date feeling really connected to each other and to God. We felt "in synch" with each other, and though the next months of transition were hectic and sometimes confusing, we could look back to our "day of prayer" and know that the God who answers prayer was still in control.

What is concerning you at this moment? Have you shared your concerns with your mate? Why not take the time right now to plan your own Prayer Date? You may want to review the exercise on page 171 in Chapter 10 and incorporate your marriage prayer list into your date. A Prayer Date will bring your marriage tracks closer together and closer to your heavenly Father!

10. Have a Bookstore Date

Maybe it's because we are authors, but we both love books and bookstores! So a Bookstore Date suits us. Our favorite Bookstore Date was a couple of years ago when we were on our own just-for-two getaway in a small town in the Colorado Rockies. In this little town was a most unusual bookstore—it even contained a little tea room where we lunched among the books.

After you make it through *The Marriage Track*, a Bookstore Date may be appropriate. Why not choose a topic—we suggest marriage enrichment—and see what creative books you can uncover? In Chapter 6 you chose your own marriage goals. You may want to take that specific emphasis (for instance, communication, sex, or managing finances) and pick out a book to read together.

If you're looking for more general marriage enrichment, we suggest the following books:

60 One-Minute Marriage Builders, Dave and Claudia
   Arp (Nashville: Wolgemuth & Hyatt, 1989).
Passages of Marriage, Dr. Frank and Mary Alice
   Minirth, Dr. Brian and Dr. Debbi Newman, and Dr.
   Robert and Susan Hemfelt (Nashville: Nelson, 1991).
The Marriage Builder, Lawrence J. Crabb (Grand
   Rapids: Zondervan, 1982).
Creating Dating, Doug Fields and Todd Temple
   (Nashville: Oliver-Nelson, 1986).
How to Have a Happy Marriage, David and Vera Mace
   (Nashville: Abingdon, 1977).
52 Simple Ways to Say I Love You, Steve Arterburn
   and Carl Dreizler (Nashville: Oliver-Nelson, 1991).

Don't overlook reading about other topics. One couple we know enjoy reading together about Civil War history. They take turns reading through novels. For instance, the book *Lonesome Dove* made for three months of evening time together.

Coming Soon: 52 Ways to Date Your Mate

If you have enjoyed *The Marriage Track* and especially this last section, perhaps you will be interested in our newest book soon to be released, *52 Ways to Date Your Mate.* It contains more creative and fun suggestions for building your marriage team.

We hope these pages have helped you get your marriage on track. Let us encourage you to keep on having an intentional marriage. Don't panic if your marriage team accidentally jumps track or temporarily derails. That only happens to those who are moving. Now you have the resources to get your marriage back on track and keep it there, and as you do just that, you'll find your marriage team will be heading in the right direction!

- -

COUPON

GOOD FOR ONE DATE WITH YOUR MATE

Fill in: Description of Date _____

_____

_____

Redeem by: _____

Time of date: Month _____ Day _____

- -

COUPON

GOOD FOR ONE DATE WITH YOUR MATE

Fill in: Description of Date _____

_____

_____

Redeem by: _____

Time of date: Month _____ Day _____

- -

COUPON

GOOD FOR ONE DATE WITH YOUR MATE

Fill in: Description of Date _____

_____

_____

Redeem by: _____

Time of date: Month _____ Day _____

- -

- -

COUPON

GOOD FOR ONE DATE WITH YOUR MATE

Fill in: Description of Date _____

_____

_____

Redeem by: _____

Time of date: Month _____ Day _____

- -

COUPON

GOOD FOR ONE DATE WITH YOUR MATE

Fill in: Description of Date _____

_____

_____

Redeem by: _____

Time of date: Month _____ Day _____

- -

COUPON

GOOD FOR ONE DATE WITH YOUR MATE

Fill in: Description of Date _____

_____

_____

Redeem by: _____

Time of date: Month _____ Day _____

- -

COUPON

GOOD FOR ONE DATE WITH YOUR MATE

Fill in: Description of Date _____

_____

_____

Redeem by: _____

Time of date: Month _____ Day _____

- -

COUPON

GOOD FOR ONE DATE WITH YOUR MATE

Fill in: Description of Date _____

_____

_____

Redeem by: _____

Time of date: Month _____ Day _____

- -

COUPON

GOOD FOR ONE DATE WITH YOUR MATE

Fill in: Description of Date _____

_____

_____

Redeem by: _____

Time of date: Month _____ Day _____

- -

TRACKING TOGETHER

Ten Dates for Mates

Purpose:
　To have fun as a couple
　To plan and have dates with your mate

Preparation:
　Review Chapter 11, "Ten Dates for Mates"
　Take turns choosing (or together choose) a date that
　　sounds fun for you and schedule it!

Our first date is:
　Fill out a coupon for your first date.

What needs to be done to make it happen:

　　1. _____
　　2. _____
　　3. _____

On actual date:
　Have fun!

NOTES

Chapter Two   Making Your Marriage a High Priority

1. Adapted from Dave Arp and Claudia Arp, *60 One-Minute Marriage Builders* (Nashville: Wolgemuth & Hyatt, 1989), 85–86.

Chapter Three   Finding Unity in Diversity

1. The Myers-Briggs Type Indicator is available through Consulting Psychologists Press, Inc., 577 College Avenue, Palo Alto, CA 94306. The Taylor-Johnson Temperament Analysis is available from Psychology Publications, 5300 Hollywood Blvd., L.A., CA 90027. Marital Evaluation Checklist ℗ is available from Psychological Assessment Resources, Inc., P.O. Box 998, Odessa, FL 33556.
2. Linda Dillow, *Creative Counterpart* (Nashville: Thomas Nelson, 1977), adapted from pp. 82–87. Used with permission of publisher.

Chapter Four   Communicating Our Feelings

1. Alan Loy McGinniss, *The Friendship Factor: How to Get Closer to the People You Care For* (Minneapolis: Augsburg, 1979), 103–104.
2. Four Styles of Communication are adapted from Training Workshop with David and Vera Mace, Association of Couples in Marriage Enrichment (A.C.M.E.), 502 North Broad Street, P.O. Box 10596, Winston-Salem, NC 27108.
3. William G. Clarke, *Marriage* (6505 N. Himes Ave., Tampa, Florida 33614: Marriage and Family Enrichment Institutes, 1974), 13.

Chapter Six   Setting Goals for Your Marriage

1. Mary Susan Miller, "What Are Your Expectations from Marriage?" *Family Life Today*, Oct. 1980, 19.
2. Ibid.
3. David Mace and Vera Mace, *We Can Have Better Marriages if We Really Want Them* (Nashville: Abingdon, 1974), 76.

Chapter Eight   Working with Your Working Mate

1. Leslie Dreyfous, "Family Finances Are Sophisticated Family Affair," *Knoxville News-Sentinel*, 9 June 1991, D–7.
2. To purchase *Manage Your Money*, write MECA Software, Inc., 327 Riverside Avenue, P.O. Box 907, Westport, CT 06881.

Chapter Nine   Getting Back on When You Jump Track

1. David Mace, *Close Companions* (New York: Continuum, 1982), 85.
2. Adapted from David Mace, *Love and Anger in Marriage* (Grand Rapids: Zondervan, 1982), 109–112.

Chapter Ten   Building a Christian Marriage

1. David Mace and Vera Mace, *The Sacred Fire* (Nashville: Abingdon, 1986), 67.

ABOUT THE AUTHORS

Dave and Claudia have been married for thirty years and are parents of three adult sons, two daughters-in-law, and five grandkittens.

Together the Arps founded and now direct Marriage Alive International, a marriage and family enrichment ministry. The Marriage Alive Workshop is popular across the United States and in Europe. They also founded the MOM'S and DAD'S Support Groups, which have curriculae for churches and schools.

Claudia is the founder of the MOM's Support Groups, a family enrichment resource program with groups throughout the United States and in Europe. She is also the author of *Beating the Winter Blues* and *Almost 13*. Claudia has a B.S. in Home Economics Education from University of Georgia.

Dave is co-author with Claudia of the *60 One-Minute Marriage Builders* and a family life educator with a B.S. from Georgia Institute of Technology and an M.S. in Social Work from the University of Tennessee.

Resources Available from Marriage Alive

Marriage Track Leader's Guide

Want to start your own marriage Track Growth Group? The Marriage Track Leader's Guide, available through Marriage Alive, gives you the nuts and bolts of how to facilitate your own small group.

Marriage Alive Workshop

The Marriage Alive Workshop with Dave and Claudia Arp is a 6 hour seminar to help you fine tune your marriage and get your marriage on track. For information about how your church or organization can host this helpful workshop contact Marriage Alive International.

Building Positive Relationships
for the Adolescent Years

This versatile program includes a five-part video series, a Leader's Guide and Parent's individual study book. MOM's & DAD's Support Group is being used by churches, schools, and groups across the country, to help parents get ready for and survive the adolescent years.

The MOM's & DAD's Support Group concept will help build a foundation for relationships every parent needs for themselves and their children.
    Jerry White/President of The Navigators/Colorado Springs, CO

Building Positive Relationships with Children

MOM's Support Groups is a video-based family enrichment resource that is providing moms with supportive friendships and helping them build positive relationships with their children. MOM's is being used by churches and small groups across the United States and in Europe to help moms enjoy motherhood while they live through it.

Endorsers of MOM's Support Group include: Josh McDowell, Dr. D. James Kennedy and Drs. David and Vera Mace.

**For more information about these and other
Marriage Alive Resources contact:**
Marriage Alive International, Inc.
P.O. Box 90303, Knoxville, TN 37990
Telephone: (615) 691-MOMS or 691-8505
Fax: (615) 691-1575